A Reader's Guide to

Modern
British
Drama

Other Reader's Guides published by Syracuse University Press

A Reader's Guide to Charles Dickens. Philip Hobsbaum

A Reader's Guide to Dylan Thomas. William York Tindall

A Reader's Guide to Ernest Hemingway. Arthur Waldhorn

A Reader's Guide to Finnegans Wake. William York Tindall

A Reader's Guide to Geoffrey Chaucer. Muriel Bowden

A Reader's Guide to Herman Melville. James E. Miller, Jr.

A Reader's Guide to James Joyce. William York Tindall

A Reader's Guide to John Milton. Marjorie Hope Nicolson

A Reader's Guide to Joseph Conrad. Frederick R. Karl

A Reader's Guide to Marcel Proust. Milton Hindus

A Reader's Guide to Modern American Drama. Sanford Sternlicht

A Reader's Guide to Modern Irish Drama. Sanford Sternlicht

A Reader's Guide to Samuel Beckett. Hugh Kenner

A Reader's Guide to the Contemporary English Novel. Frederick R. Karl

A Reader's Guide to T. S. Eliot: A Poem by Poem Analysis. George Williamson

A Reader's Guide to Walt Whitman. Gay Wilson Allen

A Reader's Guide to William Butler Yeats. John Unterecker

A Reader's Guide to William Faulkner: The Novels. Edmond Volpe

A Reader's Guide to William Faulkner: The Short Stories. Edmond Volpe

Six Metaphysical Poets: A Reader's Guide. George Williamson

A Reader's Guide to

Modern British Drama

Sanford Sternlicht

Syracuse University Press

Copyright © 2004 by Syracuse University Press
Syracuse, New York 13244–5160

All Rights Reserved

First Edition 2004

04 05 06 07 08 09   6 5 4 3 2 1

The paper used in this publication meets the minimum requirements
of American National Standard for Information Sciences–Permanence
of Paper for Printed Library Materials, ANSI Z39.48–1984.∞™

Library of Congress Cataloging–in–Publication Data
Sternlicht, Sanford V.
A reader's guide to modern British drama / Sanford
Sternlicht. – 1st ed.
p. cm.
Includes bibliographical references and index.
ISBN 0-8156-3076-X (pbk. : alk. paper)
1. English drama–20th century–History and
criticism–Handbooks, manuals, etc.   I. Title: Modern British
drama.   II. Title.
PR736.S74 2004   822'.9109–dc22 2004018690

Manufactured in the United States of America

Contents

Sanford Sternlicht was the chair of the Theater Department of the State University of New York at Oswego for twelve years. He now teaches drama theory and dramatic literature in the English Department of Syracuse University. His books on drama include *A Reader's Guide to Modern Irish Drama, A Reader's Guide to Modern American Drama,* and *Selected Plays of Padraic Colum.* He also has coedited with Christopher Fitz-Simmon *New Plays from the Abbey Theatre: 1993–1995,* and with Judy Friel, *New Plays from the Abbey Theatre: 1996–1998* and *New Plays from the Abbey Theatre: 1999–2001.* All are published with Syracuse University Press.

Acknowledgments

My thanks to my research assistants, Michelle Ley, Scott Herbst, and Aaron Metosky. Thanks also to Dr. Wendy Bousfield of Syracuse University Library for ordering many of the books I needed to complete this study. Most of all, I thank my partner, Mary Beth Hinton, for editorial advice and patient, ongoing editing of the manuscript of this book.

Backgrounds

1

The Nineteenth-Century Inheritance

In the nineteenth century, actor–managers controlled the production of plays on the London stage. Stars like Henry Irving commissioned plays that had fat roles for them. A fawning resident company provided the necessary support for the lead. Playwrights were paid a fixed sum for their scripts and all box office receipts went to the managers. Only a few bankable writers, such as the Irish–born Dion Boucicault (1822–1890), master of the melodrama, could demand and receive percentages of the take.

Although the playwright Thomas William Robertson (1829–1871) introduced realism onto the British stage with dramas like *Caste* in 1867, it was not until the work of two playwrights, Henry Arthur Jones (1852–1929) and Arthur Wing Pinero (1855–1934), that realism took hold. Influenced by Continental realism and naturalism, Jones and Pinero, together with such followers as George Bernard Shaw, began to liberate their craft by writing plays designed not as showcases for a few stars but as serious social dramas and witty comedies with credible English characters. In 1885, with *The Magistrate*, Pinero broke with the nineteenth–century comic tradition of rigidly constructed French farces with snippets of "naughty" dialogue and audience-tickling buffoonery. From then on, through the twentieth century into the present, British comedy became very British in characterization, situation, and wit.

Pinero's influence was even more significant in the area of serious drama. Just as Ibsen's new problem plays were being talked about in Britain, Pinero's *The Profligate* brought social drama to the British stage. As with his innovation in comedy, each of Pinero's problem plays illuminated a distinctly English subject. Pinero's most influential play, *The Second Mrs Tanqueray*, first performed in 1893, focused on the much–debated question of whether a "fallen woman" could ever be redeemed in polite society, and whether a man's earlier sexual transgressions were as wrong and debilitating as a woman's. These questions reflected a major social issue of the day: the limited legal rights of married women to divorce, to keep custody of children, to own property–indeed to have a legal identity. Pinero's social dramas would not have been performed in their time if not for the Independent Theatre of J. T. Grein (1862–1935), which, in 1891, began to avoid government censorship by performing controversial plays in a private club.

Although he started his playwriting career in 1882 with a very popular melodrama, *The Silver King*, Henry Arthur Jones came to be regarded as a playwright of serious plays on serious themes and moved to the forefront of socially relevant drama. He, like Pinero, attacked the double standard, but Jones also took on religious hypocrisy in *Saints and Sinners* (1884), and in many of his dramas he made it clear that he thought right and wrong are neither obvious nor clearly discernable in real life.

Henry Arthur Jones joined Pinero in attempting to write comedy that was clearly English in settings, characters, themes, and values, but he lacked Pinero's sophistication and was less successful. Beginning in 1882 Jones, talking to the periodicals of the day, fiercely advocated the cause of serious drama on the English stage. He argued that popular taste for melodramas and pantomimes demeaned what should be a national art. Indeed, he strove for the establishment of a national theater and for community theaters throughout the British Isles. Drama was to be a medium and the stage a platform for national debates on the political, social, and moral issues of the day. Most significantly, Jones wanted recognition for contemporary English drama as literature, to be taught in the schools and universities as Shakespeare was taught. If that happened, he argued, plays would be more likely than fiction to be read by the general reading public.

At the end of the nineteenth century, what was called the New Drama gave birth to modern British drama. These plays embraced realism and social themes. The movement lasted from 1892 to 1914. It began with Shaw's *Widowers' Houses* in 1892 and reached its apex in the tenures of Harley Granville-Barker (1877–1946) and J. E. Vedrenne (1867–1930) as producers at the Royal Court Theatre from 1904 to 1907. The Stage Society, founded in 1899, gave the twentieth century a legacy for the performance of English and Continental experimental plays.

Early modern British drama also inherited the concept of the "well-made play" from the nineteenth century. Originating in French drama, the well-made play (a term that in the mid-twentieth century was used in derision) is a formulaic play in which plot takes precedence over characterization. Action focuses on surprise and suspense as the hero's fortune rises and falls and rises again. The hero usually has a chief adversary who is defeated in the end. Misunderstandings between lovers or between a hero or heroine and a parent–resolved of course before the final curtain–also helped propel this carefully structured and very popular dramatic form, a form dedicated to a thrill a minute.

2

Modernism and the Drama

Modern drama is international. It had its origins in the European intellectual, aesthetic, and cultural movement now called modernism. Modern drama's staple mode is realism, which in its extreme form is referred to as naturalism. The dramatic tenets of realism and naturalism include the integration of character with environment as well as motivated action that permits the exploration of political or social dynamics. Even though modernism is primarily sited in the twentieth century, it is not a matter of epoch as much as it is a cultural and stylistic rejection of Victorian values. Modernism also both reflects and critiques the technological and social changes of the twentieth century. Trends in drama in Great Britain were influenced by the work of several major foreign playwrights.

Because of the work of the Norwegian dramatist Henrik Ibsen (1828–1906), modernism came earlier to the drama than to art, literature, music, and dance, whose modernistic forms were conceived in the first quarter of the twentieth century. Ibsen's seminal and most provocative drama is *The Doll's House* (1878), in which a middle-class wife is treated like a loveable but brainless pet by her patriarchal husband. When, in a family crisis, she is subjected to vicious verbal abuse by her selfish and ungrateful husband, she realizes that she has had no life of her own, and that she cannot love a man who does not truly respect her as a person. In an ending that shocked the theatergoing public of the Western world, Nora, the wife, walks out on her husband and children to find self-respect and a new life for herself. With that play and others, Ibsen created social drama or thesis drama in which contemporary societal problems, such as venereal disease (*Ghosts*) or the rapaciousness of community leaders who place profit above public safety (*An Enemy of the People*), are highlighted for public view, debate, and instruction.

As the new mode spread throughout the European continent and on to Britain and America, social drama irrevocably changed world drama. In Sweden, August Strindberg (1849–1912) focused on dimensions of the war between the sexes in searing realistic dramas like *The Father* and *Miss Julie*, in which European critics and intelligentsia found evidence of and support for their new fascination with the nascent psychoanalytic theories of Sigmund Freud (1856–1939). A new audience watched in simultaneous excitement and disapprobation as Strindberg's misogynistic dramas and sexually driven characters brought to light their private fears and fantasies.

The Irish playwright George Bernard Shaw brought modern drama to Britain. His dramatic output was directed toward the London stage and not the stage of his native Dublin where a great modern nationalistic drama was developing under the aegis of Lady Augusta Gregory (1852–1932), William Butler Yeats (1865–1939), and John Millington Synge (1871–1909). Shaw adapted Ibsenism and social drama to comedy, and in such plays as *Widowers' Houses*, *Mrs Warren's Profession*, *Arms and the Man*, *Major Barbara*, and *Saint Joan*, this ardent Fabian socialist engaged with such social issues as the abuse of the poor by slum landlords, the evil and corruption engendered by prostitution, the role of institutionalized religion, political corruption, clerical hypocrisy, militarism, women's suffrage, the "threat" of the independent New Woman, and the dangers of believing in the myths of history. Shaw brought the drama of ideas to the British stage, and for that reason he and his work are given the starting position in the "Playwrights and Plays" section of *A Reader's Guide to Modern British Drama.*

The tenets of modern drama reached Russia through the plays of Anton Chekhov (1860–1904). In a naturalistic mode, Chekhov eschewed the Aristotelian centrality of plot and depicted the psychologically tormented lives of upper–middle-class people who substitute talk for action, and whose seemingly pointless lives are filled with ennui and paralyzing depression. Chekhov seems to have foreshadowed the coming destruction of the idle Russian upper middle class and aristocracy in such tragicomedies as *The Seagull,· Uncle Vanya, The Three Sisters,* and *The Cherry Orchard.*

In Italy, Luigi Pirandello (1867–1936) questioned the nature of reality. In his plays, reality is relative, cognition is subjective and informed by emotion, and individuals always have personal versions of the truth. Scientific inquiry, supposedly reliable, is not infallible. In such dramas as *Right You Are–If You Think You Are, Six Characters in Search of an Author,* and *Henry IV,* Pirandello shows that our private universe is illogical. Madness or fantasy may be the only ways to escape from a corrupt modern world not worth living in.

Eugene O'Neill (1888–1953) brought modern drama to the American stage. He was perhaps the first American playwright to do profound battle with ideas. A modernist who saw life as tragic and without hope, he nevertheless wrestled with humankind's pitiless fate. He believed that men and women needed emotional catharsis to ease the burdens of life, and he strove to provide that catharsis in his dark dramas. Unlike the major earlier modernists, O'Neill was an experimenter, writing realistic, naturalistic, classical, expressionistic, and autobiographical dramas. His *Long Day's Journey into Night,* the story of a tormented Irish–American family, is one of the greatest dramatic works of the twentieth century.

Bertolt Brecht (1898–1956), Germany's master of modern drama, brought epic theater to the twentieth-century stage. Using large casts, multiple scenes, songs and placards, anarchic staging, and the mechanics of performance to keep the audience aware that they were seeing a play or perhaps witnessing a political demonstration, Brecht inculcated his socialist views. Brecht and Shaw had the same goal: to make the audience understand and reject the unjust socioeconomic conditions of the capitalist world. Brecht, a Marxist ideologue, purposely made the bourgeois audience uncomfortable; Shaw slipped his Fabian socialist message over in laughter. Brecht's plays, notably *The Threepenny Opera* (with music by Kurt Weill [1900–1950]), *Mother Courage and Her Children, Galileo, The Good Woman of Setzuan,* and *The Caucasian Chalk Circle,* showed the world how brutal and how brave, how venal and how noble, human beings can be.

Samuel Beckett (1906–1989) was born, raised, and educated in Ireland, but spent most of his life in France. He wrote mostly in French. Beckett's major tragicomedies, *Waiting for Godot, Endgame,* and *Happy Days,* are minimalist, disturbing, and pessimistic about the human condition and the future of humankind. *Waiting for Godot,* the first play of the Theater of the Absurd, is perhaps the most influential drama of the twentieth century. The ideas of post–World War II existentialism informed Beckett's work: humans are always isolated; communication is impossible; life has no purpose except the struggle to exist; and nothing transcends the boundaries of human experience.

British dramatists of the twentieth century into the twenty-first, whether writing tragedy, comedy, or tragicomedy, have been aware of the collective Western dramatic inheritance provided by these masters of modern drama. Abandoning the formulaic nineteenth-century "well-made play"–in which initial exposition is followed by sudden reversals and the buildup of tension in a central conflict brought to closure with an ending that is sometimes surprising, often improbable, but always satisfying–most of them have instead emphasized character development and examined social and psychological questions.

3

Themes and Politics in Modern British Drama

All plays are political in that they are cultural products and what is produced generally comes from and supports the culture that made it. If the play is ancient and its overt or implied message is mute, then the contemporary production will serve to either support or subvert the dominant culture of the day. Playwrights setting out to write political drama, to unite audiences in support of their specific platforms, usually do so to undermine the power structure or to attack a smug, imperfect society oblivious of its injustices. The political drama-tist may woo the audience with wit and humor as Shaw did, or alienate it by attacking it directly as Brecht did. In commercial theater it is the middle–class audience–representing the status quo–that is either castigated or cajoled.

George Bernard Shaw, an Irishman writing for the British stage, used his talents to advance the cause of Fabian socialism. As a playwright he could reach and convince far more people than he possibly could from a platform in Hyde Park. Shaw bat-tled for women's suffrage and equal rights. But foolishly roman-tic women received their due punishment in his plays. He argued for better government. He attacked the arrogance of the medical profession and the hypocrisy of the clergy. He showed how Britain exploited Ireland and how the Irish were complicit in the process. Warriors, capitalists, and munitions makers were excoriated. Shaw made war on the vapidity and self-absorption of the British aristocracy. Having observed urban poverty and unemployment during the Great Depression, Shaw distrusted parliamentary democracy as a means of bringing equality to British society. Most of all, Shaw strove to smash conformity and energize the moral sense he believed inherent in most human beings.

As for "the Irish question," Shaw made it clear in *John Bull's Other Island* (1904) that he saw no resolution to England's continual capitalist exploitation of Ireland and the participation of many Irish people in that process. He saw in the two countries a prevalence of impractical dreamers and a paucity of practical doers.

John Galsworthy's liberal politics pervaded his social dramas. They expressed his view that wealth often bought "justice" and that gargantuan struggles between labor and management seldom brought about significant reform. More radically, other playwrights damned business in the 1920s for its complete lack of morality in the search for profits, a search that would even condone war if it made money for the firm.

In 1956 the political discourse prompted by the production of John Osborne's *Look Back in Anger* at the Royal Court Theatre radicalized British drama. It was fueled in part by the new audience: young men and women, students mostly, who sensed that the theater was no longer moribund—merely a comfortable outing for smug, middle-aged, bourgeois patrons— but moving in new directions. The young adopted a socialist political outlook, directing their anger against the power of the establishment, censorship, sexual repression, the proliferation of nuclear weapons, conscription, and the general ennui of the British public. The Anglo–French imperialist fiasco at the Suez Canal in 1956 confirmed suspicions held by many, if not most, young Britons that the older generation was inept and corrupt.

If the working class was not exactly rushing to buy tickets to the new social drama, perhaps best exemplified by Arnold Wesker's late-1950s trilogy about socialist values under fire– *Chicken Soup with Barley, Roots,* and *I'm Talking about Jerusalem*–it was now at least welcome in the British theater and able to find characters and experiences that workers could relate to. In derision the new plays were called "kitchen sink drama" because of the tenement settings of the plays–often the kitchen of an urban flat that also served as the family living room. The term is now used descriptively and without ridicule.

Two new themes emerged in British drama: the alienation of the young and the belief that class warfare was endemic, pervading, and would lead to radical changes in British society.

In 1928 antiwar drama appeared with R. C. Sherriff's *Journey's End,* depicting the soldier's miserable life in the battle zone. Antiwar drama began as a belated reaction to the slaughter in the trenches of World War I. It was a part of the popular peace movement of the period between the two world wars.

At the end of the 1950s, the British campaign for nuclear disarmament began, a reaction to the nuclear arms race between the United States and the Soviet Union. Left-leaning Royal Court playwrights like John Osborne and Arnold Wesker and the critic Kenneth Tynan were to be found marching with the demonstrators.

In the 1960s many Britons began to protest American actions in Vietnam. In 1968 mass demonstrations supporting the Viet Cong not only incited anti-Americanism but also revitalized the peace movement in the United Kingdom. One of the most successful of British drama's contributions to the peace movement was Joan Littlewood's *Oh, What a Lovely War!,* first produced in 1963 and later made into a film by Richard Attenborough in 1969. The drama, with songs of the World War I period, depicts the folly of war brought about by rulers and diplomats and run by incompetent generals.

The government of Harold Wilson in the 1960s brought disillusionment with the Labour Party by those on the far left who had once been Labour's most ardent supporters. Young Britons still embraced socialism but no longer respected Soviet Communism because of its cruelties and corruption. They began to form the New Left—more radical than Labour. Many found that the theater expressed their antiestablishment values, disappointments, fears, and anger better than the political cant on TV and radio. In the late 1950s and through the 1970s John Arden and Edward Bond used drama to illustrate the struggle individuals must endure in what these social dramatists saw as a regimenting, unjust, and predatory society. Plays like Arden's *Serjeant Musgrave's Dance* and Bond's *Saved* used shocking theatrical imagery to wave the red flag in the faces of startled audiences.

The marginalization of British industrial workers beginning in the 1970s sparked the work of socially conscious playwrights such as Howard Brenton, Howard Barker, David Hare, and David Edgar who were determined to make the Margaret Thatcher-supporting bourgeois audience aware of what postindustrial and early globalization life was like for the working class.

Savaging what they saw as a decadent and decaying British society in the 1970s and 1980s, the playwrights Trevor Griffiths, Howard Brenton, and Howard Barker, sometimes employing black humor, dramatized class hatred in agitprop plays.

From the 1970s and continuing into the twenty-first century, British feminist and gay and lesbian writers have used the theater as a political platform for their ongoing and succeeding campaign for civil rights, equal opportunities, and societal acceptance.

4

Feminist Drama and Gay Drama

Generally speaking, feminist drama arose in alternative theatrical venues in the early 1970s in parallel with the gay liberation movement in Britain. Its emergence was made possible by the elimination of stage censorship in 1968. Female playwrights were few in number in modern British drama from its beginning until 1958. In that year *A Taste of Honey*, written by the nineteen-year-old Shelagh Delaney and directed by Joan Littlewood, brought the first indications of a feminine consciousness and a feminist agenda to the British stage. In 1973 the Women's Theatre Festival was held at London's Almost Free Theatre. With women performing almost all of the production roles, it was a landmark event in the gender history of Great Britain. As the women's movement and gay liberation continued in the 1970s, women's drama organizations, such as the Women's Theatre Group and the Women's Company, blossomed and flourished.

British women dramatists seem generally open to depicting gay and bisexual characters in a favorable light. Alternative lifestyles are fairly explored. Female characters predominate in feminist drama, and sometimes male characters are totally absent. Polemics, of course, are not excluded. Women dramatists are determined to put to rest the old paradigm of the traditional woman on the stage: an undervalued, economically dependent, powerless creature, expected to serve men sexually

15

and to nurture their children. These traditional female characters were despised in all their goodness while evil females were feared, hated, and usually killed off.

The feminist agenda in drama includes the demand to show real women on the stage, not merely projections of male fantasies. It insists on equal rights for women in the predominantly male departments of the theater: direction and production. In demanding fair wages for women workers, it does not forget the sisters who clean the dressing rooms, sweep the auditoriums, and do other menial tasks.

The agenda also includes creating an alternative canon of women's plays. British feminist drama battles misogyny. It shows the social reality of the relationship between the sexes. It aims at empowering women in the traditional male–dominated British society. Obviously, contemporary women's plays offer a different perspective about patriarchal society, but they are also frequently nonviolent. They neither bash nor trash the family. Women dramatists insist that gender–as well as class and race–is a determining factor in understanding the meaning of a play. They are more Brechtian than Beckettian in that they believe that social change is possible, even inevitable, especially if pushed along by their agitprop dramas.

Prostitution is a frequent subject in British feminist drama. It is seen as female exploitation in plays written by men, but in feminist drama it is sometimes presented as an example of women using their bodies for compensatory economic advantages. Women writers have embraced the history play, but their historical dramas are designed to record and register women's history.

British feminist drama not only candidly discusses sex, but it also notes the relationship between sex and power. It helps to empower women by creating a feminist dramatic canon. In the first rank of feminist dramatists are Caryl Churchill and Pam

Gems, followed by Michelene Wandor, Timberlake Werten-baker, and Sarah Daniels.

Three of the most important British dramatists of the mid-dle of the twentieth century were gay. None of them came out of the closet in their lifetime, although there was an awareness of their sexual preference in theatrical circles. Somerset Maugham wrote sardonic social satires in which marriage ap-pears very problematic and spouses frequently defy societal conventions, commit adultery, or leave to find different lives and alternate living arrangements.

Noël Coward wrote delightful social, supposedly amoral, comedies for West End audiences, in which he divided his the-atrical world into "in" and "out" people. The former live in fam-ily-free environs. Women, notably wives, generally plague men.

Terence Rattigan wrote social dramas. Although designed to please the general theatergoing public, they contain subtle pleas for understanding of the suffering of men and women seeming at odds with the gender roles they play. For example, in Rattigan's historical drama about T. E. Lawrence (Lawrence of Arabia), *Ross*, the hero learns the truth of his homosexuality from being raped by Turks who are torturing him.

Prior to the abolition of theater censorship in Britain in 1968, gay dramatists honored a "gentleman's agreement" with producers that their plays would not reveal their own lifestyles. Gay writers could only hint at homosexual activity in coded or obtuse ways so as not to shock or offend the heterosexual au-dience and perhaps drive away business. With the sexual rev-olution of the 1960s and 1970s, this duplicity was no longer an imperative.

Joe Orton's outrageously funny farces are filled with promis-cuous characters, grotesque seductions, perversions, irrever-ence, cross–dressing, and homosexual suggestion. Orton takes a fiendish delight in savaging the British family and conventional notions of heterosexual romantic love. Peter Nichols's popular satirical comedy with songs, *Privates on Parade*, about a traveling entertainment unit in the British Army in post–World War II Malaya, is a delightful camp romp with drag routines, parody, gay banter, and serious anticolonial politics. *Bent*, by Martin Sherman, an American residing in Dublin, connects the little-known Nazi persecution of homosexuals with the extermination of most of European Jewry in World War II.

In the 1970s gay theater groups, such as the Gay Street Theatre and the Gay Sweatshop, emerged. Contemporary dramatists writing on gay themes include Peter Gill, whose *Mean Tears* depicts the intense love of an intellectual for an unworthy bisexual, and Kevin Elyot, whose compassionate play *My Night with Reg* depicts the spread of AIDS among a small group of friends.

Contemporary British gay drama celebrates the full gamut of alternative homosexual lifestyles, from plays depicting gay relationships as monogamous and committed as heterosexual ones to plays demonstrating a lighthearted adoration of camp in all its inimitable, funky, in-your-face, "queer"ness. Of course, much gay drama laments partners and pals lost to the AIDS plague.

5

Major Directions in Modern British Theater

The great vitality and the magnificence of modern British drama are in no small measure a result of the development of a highly sophisticated theater that reflected and continues to reflect the many intellectual interests of the well-educated British public. In the twentieth century, the United Kingdom endured two devastating world wars and the loss of the largest empire the world had ever known. British society became multicultural. Great social changes broke down many class barriers. Economic changes brought about by Fabian and Marxist socialism endured. The suffrage movement brought women the vote. Feminism and gay liberation battered the walls of patriarchy and homophobia. New universities sprung up and higher education became available to more young people than anyone would have thought possible in 1900. And the British theater provided the venues and resources for modern British drama to reflect a century of unprecedented change.

An inkling of the vitality to come was the turn-of-the-century movement called the New Drama, which flourished from 1892 to 1914. It commenced with George Bernard Shaw's *Widowers' Houses*, performed in 1892 in the Independent Theatre Club (founded by Holland-born J. T. Grein), which also made it possible for controversial plays by such naturalistic dramatists as Ibsen and Strindberg to be performed in Britain. The club, being "private," was able to avoid both censorship and public criticism of "immoral" plays like Ibsen's *Ghosts*. The Independent Theatre was modeled on the Théâtre Libre of Antoine in Paris, an influential European theater devoted to the promulgation of naturalism on the stage.

From 1904 to 1907, the venue for a major part of the New Drama movement was the Royal Court Theatre in Sloane Square. Under director Harley Granville-Barker (1877–1946) and producer J. E. Vedrenne (1867–1930), the Royal Court also helped bring the continental European tide of realism and social consciousness to the English shore.

The Stage Society succeeded the Independent Theatre Club in 1899 and, starting with Shaw's *You Never Can Tell*, it gave the twentieth century a legacy for the performance of English and Continental experimental plays. It introduced playwrights Somerset Maugham and D. H. Lawrence to the British playgoing public. In 1926 the Stage Society merged with the Three Hundred Club, which had been founded in 1923. The merged organization closed in 1939, long after it had endeared performers like Laurence Olivier, Edith Evans, and Peggy Ashcroft to British audiences.

The London Gate Theatre, another theater club, opened in 1925 in a Covent Garden warehouse. Two years later it was moved to the Charing Cross district. For another dozen years the theater was the venue for exciting new Continental plays as well as important American dramas by contemporary playwrights like Lillian Hellman and John Steinbeck. German bombers destroyed the theater in 1941 and it was not rebuilt.

German bombers also ended the life of London's Little Theatre in 1941, although the remains of the building were not fully demolished until 1949. German bombs had damaged the theater in 1917 also. The Little Theatre had opened in 1910 in

what was a section of a bank. There Noël Coward made his acting debut in 1911, and in the 1920s and 1930s the Little Theatre
featured the works of contemporary British dramatists with
ideas to explore and causes to advocate.

In 1933 the Mercury Theatre opened in the Notting Hill
district in London under the direction of Ashley Dukes. In the
1950s and later, it featured experimental and poetic plays by
such British writers as W. H. Auden, Christopher Isherwood,
and Christopher Fry, as well as the American Eugene O'Neill.

Also in 1933 the Group Theatre in London was established
under Rupert Doone largely to present English poetic drama
by such modern poets as T. S. Eliot, W. H. Auden, and Stephen
Spender. The Group Theatre struggled until finally closing in
the 1950s.

London's first communist theater was founded near King's
Cross in 1936. It moved to St. Pancras in 1937. It specialized in
the plays of Brecht, Sean O'Casey, and other leftist dramatists. It
survived as something of a political dinosaur until a fire destroyed the theater in 1975.

The Old Vic Theatre first opened in 1818 on the South Bank
of the Thames River near Waterloo Bridge. It is one of the oldest theaters in the world. It was first named the Royal Coburg
Theatre, and over its nearly two hundred years of existence it
has had several other names. Before World War II, the Old Vic
dramatic company included the distinguished actors Lawrence
Olivier, John Gielgud, and Ralph Richardson. The theater suffered bomb damage in the 1941 Blitz and did not open again
until 1950. The Old Vic Company, after over a decade of glory,
was disbanded in 1963 and the National Theatre Company
took over the venue until 1976.

In the interim, the Prospect Theatre Company–founded in
Oxford in 1961 and moved to Cambridge in 1964–became the
Old Vic Company. It was dedicated to innovative Shake-

spearean productions. Some of the finest British actors of the time, including Derek Jacobi, Ian McKellen, Peter O'Toole, and Dorothy Tutin, performed in the company. The Old Vic Company had to disband when it lost its government arts funding in 1980, but the theater continued to mount successful productions through the 1980s. The Old Vic sparkled during a brief residency–1996–97–by the Peter Hall Company, but it then went temporarily dark. At this writing in 2003, the grand old theater is flourishing under the management of the American actor Kevin Spacey.

The Young Vic Theatre, with five hundred seats, was founded by Frank Dunlop in 1970 near the Old Vic. It has aimed at a young audience with its lively productions and less expensive tickets.

Joan Littlewood's Theatre Workshop in East London was founded in 1945. It ultimately settled in the London working-class suburb of Stratford East in what had been a Victorian theater called the Theatre Royal. This experimental organization introduced and molded the work of Shelagh Delaney and the Irish playwright Brendan Behan. The innovative style of Theatre Workshop productions was based on the Brechtian model, the best example of which is *Oh, What a Lovely War!*, staged in 1963. The Stage Sixty Company occupied the theater from 1964 to 1967, but Littlewood returned to lead the company until 1973. Refurbished in 2000, the theater continues to stage avant-garde plays.

In 1956 George Devine founded the English Stage Company. It performed at the Royal Court Theatre. Its mission was to promote new English dramatists and plays. The production of John Osborne's *Look Back in Anger* in the company's first year marked the introduction of a new political theater in the United Kingdom in which disaffected youth took on the complacent establishment. To this day the Royal Court Theatre continues to be one of the most exciting and innovative theaters in Britain.

The Shakespeare Memorial Theatre was founded in 1879 in Stratford–upon–Avon. From 1886 to 1926 the annual Shakespeare Festival plays were performed in a Gothic-style edifice. When a fire destroyed the theater in 1926, the present building went up, opening in 1932. In 1960 the distinguished director Peter Hall took charge. He formed the Royal Shakespeare Company (RSC). The theater was renamed the Royal Shakespeare Theatre. In 1963 the RSC also established itself in London, dividing its time between Stratford–upon–Avon and the capital. It is one of the two leading dramatic companies in Britain today; the other is the National Theatre Company. The RSC has had triumphant international tours and smash hits on Broadway too. Three great directors, Peter Hall, Peter Brook, and Trevor Nunn, students of Brecht and Beckett, have made the RSC one of the most innovative theatrical enterprises in the world. In 1982 the company moved into its permanent London venue, the Barbican, with one large and one studio theater space.

The Donmar Warehouse Theatre began in an interesting location–in the vat room of a former Covent Garden brewery that also was once used for the storage of bananas. In 1977 it became the Royal Shakespeare Company's studio theater until 1982. Since 1992, despite being very small, the Donmar has turned out critically acclaimed and popular productions of new plays, experimental drama, musicals, and classics, under the leadership of the artistic director, Sam Mendes.

The British began discussing the idea of a national theater in the middle of the nineteenth century. In the first decade of the twentieth century the debate became quite heated, but still nothing was actually accomplished. Finally, and oddly enough in the midst of World War II (1944), a site was designated on the

South Bank of the Thames River near Waterloo Bridge, and an architect was appointed. Eighteen years later the National Theatre Board was created and Lawrence Olivier became the first artistic director of the National Theatre Company. The company moved into the Old Vic Theatre on a temporary basis when the Old Vic Company dissolved. Fourteen years later, in 1976, the magnificent new three-theater complex opened on the South Bank. In 1988 the National Theatre became the Royal National Theatre.

Feminist, gay, and lesbian images began to move into the mainstream of British theater in the 1970s, having first been conceived in fringe venues. In 1975 Monstrous Regiment was established to revise the patriarchal image of women on stage. Other feminist companies include Mrs Worthington's Daughter (from a disparaging line in a Noël Coward song) and the Sphinx Theatre Company. In 1975 the Gay Sweatshop was founded in London with a primary political mission to support the struggle for equal rights for homosexuals.

Portable Theatre was founded by the playwright David Hare in 1968 to perform drama from the left attacking social privilege and a complacent bourgeois British society. It was one of several, often short-lived, fringe theaters with radical or revolutionary agendas. The 1970s were their most successful years. To the credit of the British government, the fringe groups were aided by funds from the Arts Council. Mainly, the fringe served as a useful and important socialist antidote to West End theater.

Fringe companies and venues included the Welfare State, founded in 1968 as an experimental theater and lasting into the 1990s; the General Will; the Pip Simons Theatre Group, founded in London in 1968 to do plays based on literary classics and surviving outside of Britain until 1986; Red Ladder, founded in 1972 and named for a prop; the Bush Theatre, founded in 1972 in the Shepherd's Bush district of London; and

the Joint Stock Theatre, also founded by Hare in 1974 to perform social drama and feminist plays such as Caryl Churchill's
A Mouthful of Birds. It began operating as a touring company in
1974 to bring thoughtful and provocative plays to the nation
outside of London, and it survived almost twenty years, making it one of the longest lived of the avant–garde radical fringe
theater companies.

In 1971 John McGrath's 7:84 Company was named for the
fact that seven percent of the British population owned eighty-
four percent of the nation's wealth, a statistic that would have
driven a furious Brecht to his writing table. The major playwrights who came out of this passionately radical agitprop theater scene included David Hare, Howard Brenton, David Edgar,
Howard Barker, Trevor Griffiths, and John McGrath. Their ultimate target was widespread corruption in British society, the
decline of respect for the workforce, and the indifference of the
government to the poor. Their audience was both the bourgeoisie and the working class, the former to develop a social
conscience and the latter to learn and perhaps take action.

In 1986 the actor Kenneth Branagh of the Royal Shakespeare Company founded the Renaissance Theatre Company in
an apparent attempt to bring back the old actor–manager
regime that dominated nineteenth–century drama. The company has specialized in Shakespearean plays and revivals of
English classics. Branagh also directed and acted in his own
play, *Tell Me Honestly*.

Opening in 1997 under the artistic director and actor Mark
Ryland, the magnificent replica of Shakespeare's Globe Theatre
on the South Bank of the Thames has thrilled audiences with
productions of Shakespearean plays that approximate Eliza-
bethan staging. The new Globe is the realization of the great
dream of the American actor Sam Wanamaker, who began the
project in the early 1970s but did not live to see its completion.

In the first years of the twenty-first century, Shakespearean drama thrives on the British stage in several venues. Feminist drama, gay and lesbian plays, and radical agitprop theater flourishes in the variously sited festival theaters, the fringe, the great companies, the regional theaters, and even the commercial West End, while London remains the great–and some would say successful–rival of New York for the title of theater capital of the English-speaking world.

6

Historical Events, 1899–2003

The twentieth century started early for the United Kingdom of Great Britain and Ireland. In 1899 Britain decided to add to its own territories those held by the Boers (Dutch Farmers) in South Africa. To the surprise of the British Army, which since the Crimean War (1853–1856) had not fought Europeans with weapons as modern as their own, the vastly outnumbered and outgunned Boers put up a fierce resistance for their homeland, defeating several columns of British regulars and besieging fortress towns. Britain's reputation in the family of nations was greatly hurt by what much of the world saw as imperial aggression. During the war, which finally ended in 1902 with the capitulation of the Boers, the British invented the concentration camp for innocent Boer civilians, and the Boers perfected guerilla warfare. Both are terrible legacies of the twentieth century.

Queen Victoria (1819–1901), the woman who gave her name to an age, died in 1901. At the time of her death, the British Empire–thanks to the Industrial Revolution, liberal capitalism, and superior technology–sprawled across three-fourths of the surface of the earth. Every inhabited continent had British colonies or dominions. In South Asia alone, what are now India, Pakistan, Bangladesh, Sri Lanka, and Myanmar were ruled by that island off the western coast of Europe: Great Britain. A few thousand British administrators, a small professional army augmented by native troops, and the Royal Navy maintained worldwide British hegemony. After the post–World War I Treaty of Versailles in 1919, even more peoples were added to the empire.

After Victoria's death, during the nine–year reign of King Edward VII (1841–1910) and the four years after his death with King George V (1865–1936) on the throne, the United Kingdom enjoyed a period of predominance, peace, prosperity, and progress that was looked back on as the "Edwardian Summer" preceding the conflagration of World War I. The only event that seemed in retrospect to have shaken British confidence and presaged the catastrophes to come was the foundering of the Titanic in 1912.

World War I (1914–1918) ended in victory for Great Britain and her allies–France, Italy, and the United States–but the nation was exhausted by the great loss of life and the enormous war debt. No sooner had the war ended on the Continent than Ireland rebelled from seven hundred years of English rule (the initial, unsuccessful, uprising had come in 1916). The Anglo–Irish War ended in 1922 with the partition of the island into the Irish Free State–later called the Republic of Ireland–and the loyal British province of Northern Ireland. The dispute over the conditions of the Anglo–Irish Peace Treaty still cause conflict on the island of Ireland today.

The Kingdom of Great Britain and Northern Ireland entered a period of social unrest between the wars: a general strike in 1926, disarmament, pacifism, economic depression, and a constitutional crisis that in 1936 resulted in the abdication of King Edward VIII (1895–1972) only a few months after his father's death. And with the outbreak of World War II in September 1939, the country was yet again engaged in a life–and–death struggle with Germany. Under the indomitable Winston Churchill (1874–1965), Britain survived blitzkreig and blitz until the Soviet Union and the United States joined the fray in 1941. The Allied victory over Nazi Germany in 1945 left Europe devastated and Britain drained of will and wealth.

In 1952 the ascension of the young Queen Elizabeth II (1926–) upon the death of her father King George VI (1895–1952) seemed to revitalize the nation, but the Suez crisis (1956), in which Britain and France seized the canal in order to prevent its nationalization under the Egyptian government, ended in a humiliating withdrawal under pressure from the world community. That event signaled the end of Great Britain as a first-class world power as the United States and the Soviet Union rivaled for world hegemony. But during the cold war (1947–1991), Britain remained America's staunchest and most valuable ally.

The exhausted British, having given up India in 1947, no longer could either afford or control the other colonies, and a succession of partitions, withdrawals, and wars of liberation over twenty years drained the empire away. It was replaced by the British Commonwealth, a loose organization consisting of Britain, the Dominions, and many former colonies who wished to maintain economic and cultural ties. Beginning in the 1960s, large numbers of people from the former colonies emigrated to Great Britain, settling primarily in London and the industrial cities of the north, and turning Britain into a multiethnic and multicultural society.

A significant social change came to Britain after the recommendations of the 1957 Wolfenden Report on homosexuality and prostitution sparked a decade of long–overdue legislation, eventually establishing, with the Sexual Offences Act of 1967, that any sexual behavior between consenting adults in private could not be considered criminal. The closet had opened for those who chose to come out. In 1968, after some four hundred years, theater censorship was abolished in Great Britain.

The United Kingdom joined the European Economic Union (later called the European Union or EU) in 1973, bringing the nation closer to its continental neighbors than it had been since the loss of its last possessions in France during the sixteenth century. Devoid of most colonial possessions and responsibilities, and identifying more with continental Europe, the United Kingdom significantly reduced its military and naval forces despite its commitment to NATO.

In 1982, however, the British lion roared once more. The Argentine military junta, believing Great Britain no longer had the will or the power to hold the Falkland Islands, seized control of the Islands and their inhabitants, who were largely of British descent. Britain mounted a powerful relief armada that sailed over 7,000 miles to the South Atlantic where it inflicted a humiliating defeat on Argentina while freeing the islands and their English-speaking population.

A new patriotism came out of the Falkland experience, and the United Kingdom decided to rearm in order to project significant British power when necessary anywhere in the world. In the 1991 gulf war to liberate Kuwait from Iraqi conquest and in the 2003 gulf war to liberate Iraq from tyrannical rule, Great Britain stood by the United States as its chief ally. A new era of Anglo–American friendship and collaboration commenced as Americans and Britons recognized their common values, culture, and world perspective.

Playwrights and Plays

7

The First Moderns

George Bernard Shaw (1856–1950)

To many people the theater mainly serves as entertainment. A spectacular musical, a light situation comedy, or a boisterous farce is quite enough. They do not expect to be hurt or healed by what they hear and see from the stage. A play does not cause them to rush out to the street to protest. It does not lead them into war or out of it. Shaw, however, wanted people to experience theater differently from the way most of his contemporary dramatists did. He was determined to cajole at least a part of the British theatergoing audience into accepting his belief that the stage was a political platform. On it he would retail his socialist program.

Shaw was a man of principle. He very much wanted to reform the world according to his precepts and values. He had little use for those aesthetes, like his early rival and fellow Irish wit Oscar Wilde (1854–1900), who advocated art for art's sake.

Shaw's reiterated, didactic message is that people should think for themselves. He believed that his audience was intelligent. Thus wit–an appeal to the intellect through brilliant, amusing language, rather than broad, farcical humor–structures his comedy. Shaw frequently replaced or altered the traditional exposition–complication–resolution pattern of conventional drama with a construct that is both Socratic and Hegalian. In the Socratic sense, Shaw deflates conventional "wisdom" by first exposing it through the values expressed by the characters, then by gradually showing that the accepted values are really worthless and a paradoxical set of values are more sensible. Finally, Shaw indicates how the better (Shavian socialist) values can be tested and implemented. In Hegelian terms, Shaw presents as a thesis the conventional values of society, then counters them with antithetical evidence of their failures, and concludes with a synthesis that points to a new direction for an old society.

Shaw's comedy is not about funny people but about what in society is comical. Society is not rational. Humans must try to be rational (rather than emotional), but it is hard to be so in an irrational world.

Early on Shaw presented the "new woman" as heroines in his comedies. He vigorously supported women's suffrage. He was so antiwar that his career was nearly destroyed in World War I, when his plays were banished from the stage. Shaw made war on poverty. The great Shavian paradox is that poverty is the worst of all crimes in a capitalist society.

Shaw's dramaturgy could be old-fashioned or very modern. His plays often followed the well-made play formula, replete with alternations of suspense and surprise, unexpected entrances, and astonishing reversals. On the other hand, he was the first British dramatist to put an automobile and an airplane (crashed) on the stage, and to depict an air raid.

Most significantly, Shaw admired, studied, and wrote about Ibsen. His "Quintessence of Ibsenism" (1891) not only delineated the Norwegian's iconoclastic purposes in attacking hypocritical bourgeois society's values, it set an agenda for Shaw himself. Shaw was a showman and a comedian. He naturally gave social drama a comic twist, for comedy is the Irish genius, and Shaw, despite his long residence in England, always remained an Irishman. Although his plays are discussion plays, his discourse is always dramatic. Although ideas take precedence over action, his plays often surprise us. Polemics abound but the characters are true to life, if eccentric. Thus Shavian dramas, despite argumentation, cannot easily be abstracted into essays.

Shaw's dedication to Fabian socialism and his sincere desire to make the world a better place differentiated him from the apolitical naturalism of the continental modernists like Ibsen and Strindberg. And because of Shaw's overwhelming popularity and theatrical influence during the first half of the twentieth century, British drama is distinctly different from continental European drama. Even the "angry young men" and kitchen sink realists of the fifties and early sixties followed the dicta of Shaw in their social realism and political agenda. The agitprop dramatists of the seventies and eighties—in their passion for equality for women, civil rights for homosexuals, and justice for all classes—were, after all, neo-Shavians.

Shaw's paternal ancestry was predominately English. At the decisive 1689 Battle of the Boyne, in which the Protestant William II of England defeated the Catholic James II, the fate of Ireland was determined. The country would remain a British colony for another 232 years. Captain William Shaw, a Hampshire man who fought heroically on the side of William in the battle, was awarded tracts of land in County Kilkenny. For well over one hundred years the Shaw family prospered. In 1821 another of Shaw's paternal ancestors, Robert Shaw, became a baronet, but the family soon began a rapid decline until at the time of the birth of Shaw's father the Shaws were a lower-middle-class Protestant family in which the men were afflicted with alcoholism. Shaw's paternal grandfather, a stockbroker, collapsed and died after a cheating partner took off with the firm's money. He left a widow and eleven children, one of whom was Shaw's father George Carr Shaw. He became a notably unsuccessful wholesale dealer in grains.

At the age of thirty-seven, the unmarried grain dealer thought he had found a potentially wealth-bringing marriage partner. The woman who was to become Shaw's mother, Lucinda Elizabeth Gurly, age twenty-one and also Protestant, did not come directly from a wealthy family; her father was a landowner at a time when land ownership was almost more a liability than a source of profit. But Lucinda had a wealthy aunt who had helped to raise and educate her, and who promised a wedding settlement if Lucinda married wisely, preferably someone of whom the aunt approved. George Carr Shaw knew about the possible legacy. Lucinda was duped into believing that he had some money and was a prosperous businessman. They married and went to Liverpool for their honeymoon, where Lucinda quickly found out that George was an alcoholic. Their marriage was in no way a love match. Not surprisingly, the aunt, learning of George's alcoholism and shaky business, disinherited her niece. Lucinda found some solace for her unexpected genteel poverty in her children. Two daughters were followed by a son, George Bernard Shaw, born in 1856 in the family house on 3 Upper Synge Street (now 33 Synge Street), a mile away from the far more fashionable and prestigious early homes of Shaw's later rival Oscar Wilde, who had been born two years before.

Lucinda also found solace from her disastrous marriage in music. She had a good mezzo-soprano voice. Shortly before Shaw was born, she began to take singing lessons from a Svengali-like music teacher, George John Lee, a Catholic from the countryside who had come to Dublin to seek his fortune. The music teacher quickly took control of Lucinda, who may have become his lover. It has even been conjectured that Shaw was really his son, and all his life, Shaw tried to hide the nature of his mother's relationship with yet another man named George. With Shaw's dislike for the music man and his disdain for his alcoholic and improvident father, it is no wonder that the playwright hated the name George and insisted on being called Bernard Shaw.

When Shaw was ten, the family moved into a house on Hatch Street, and Lee moved in with them. Shaw's father seemed to have no objection to the arrangement, partly because expenses were shared. Shaw saw relatively little of his mother as she struggled to have a professional music career in a city not able to support many musicians. Servant girls, cheaply hired, took Shaw and his sisters in hand. Sometimes the servants, without parental permission, took Shaw to pubs where the child saw more drunkenness.

Shaw's education was mediocre. After early tutoring, at ten he began to attend the Wesleyan Connexional School in Dublin. At twelve he was placed in a school in Dalkey, the village south of Dublin where Lee owned a cottage and where the "extended" family spent summers. As money was scarce in the household, Shaw was transferred to the Central Model School in Dublin where to his horror he had to associate with working-class Catholic children. The fact that those children were Catholics did not bother Shaw as much as their working-class status: that was a sign of his family's fall. Shaw's religious faith seemed to have waned early in life. Shaw's last school was the Dublin English Scientific and Commercial Day School. Shaw was always a middling student.

So when formal schooling was over, Shaw began his self-education with reading, going as often as he could to view the art in the nearby National Gallery of Ireland, and enjoying the music his mother, sisters—who were also musicians—and Lee brought into the otherwise unhappy home. Shaw became very knowledgeable about music and even taught himself to play the violin.

Unfortunately, Shaw could not even think of seeking admission to Trinity College because he could not have passed the entrance examinations nor could his father have paid the tuition. So Shaw had to go to work at age fifteen. His first job, which he hated, was as a junior clerk in a land office.

But now the household was breaking up. George Lee moved to London. Perhaps in coordination, two weeks later Lucinda and her daughters joined Lee–who was now calling himself George John Vanderleur Lee–in the British capital where opportunities in the music field were far greater than in Dublin. The abandoned men, Shaw and his father, moved into inexpensive rented rooms not far from their previous residences.

Lucinda's younger daughter died of tuberculosis in London in 1876. Shaw decided there was now room for him in his mother's household, and he fled the miserable life with his father for the chances of a better life in London. When George Carr Shaw died in 1885 neither his wife nor his children bothered to return to Dublin for his funeral. He was a forgotten man.

In London, Bernard Shaw spent much time in the famous Reading Room of the British Museum where so many writers, philosophers, and revolutionaries had researched their books. The British Museum Library was Shaw's university. At the urging of his mother, Shaw got work in 1879 with the Edison Telephone Company, but he had already started on what he thought would be a career as a novelist. Five unpublished novels later, Shaw came to the realization that fiction would not be his literary medium.

In 1881 Shaw became a lifelong vegetarian after reading the poetry and political tracts of Percy Bysshe Shelley. His dislike for his father's alcoholism caused him to refuse drink and abhor drunkards. Shaw later attributed his good health and long life to his vegetarian diet and his lifelong abstinence from alcohol and tobacco.

Reading Marx and other economists converted Shaw to socialism, and as he had joined a debating society primarily for self-improvement, he took to oratory, preaching socialism in parks and on street corners. In 1884 Shaw joined the Fabian Society where he met intellectuals like Sidney and Beatrice Webb, William Morris, and Annie Besant. Fabian socialists believed in gradual change in the effort to improve conditions for the working class, as opposed to the Marxist socialist doctrine of forcing change through class warfare or revolution.

Shaw very much wanted to stand out. He eschewed the conventional theater dress of the time and wore a heavy wool suit. He grew a beard and turned the ends of his moustache and eyebrows up so as to look satanic. His flaming red hair helped with the impression, but his demeanor was more impish than evil. The facial hair also served to cover pitting from a childhood attack of smallpox.

Surprisingly, the confident young orator was shy and awkward when it came to women. He was twenty-nine when he had his first sexual experience. His lover was a woman closer to his mother's age than to his own. Jenny Patterson was a widow who became deeply devoted to Shaw, but he soon took an interest in other females, mainly actresses. Jenny was furious and violent. Shaw used the events of their breakup and of his subsequent philandering in his play *The Philanderer*, produced in 1905.

Shaw had met the drama critic William Archer in 1883 in the British Museum, and they had become friends. Archer helped Shaw get work as a play reviewer and as a music critic. Shaw was quite successful in those occupations, and Archer and he decided to collaborate on an Ibsen–like play. Archer lost interest and Shaw completed the play alone. Five years later, in December 1892, J. T. Grein offered two performances in the Independent Theatre Club. With *Widower's Houses*–an attack on slum landlords and a cynical play about how easy it is to compromise on principles when money and sex are involved–Shaw's destined career as a dramatist was launched. He wrote *The Philanderer* next but production was delayed, as was his third play, *Mrs Warren's Profession*, a play whose subject–the economics of prostitution–was so shocking that although it was written in 1893, it was not produced until 1902 in America and 1925 in Britain.

Arms and the Man (1894), an antiwar comedy, was Shaw's first somewhat successful play. It was well received at the first performance, but in subsequent performances the cast overplayed their characters and the subtlety was lost. Shaw took more interest in the performances of his plays after that and became an outstanding director of his own material. Now *Arms and the Man* is one of Shaw's most frequently performed and read plays.

Candida, written in 1894 but not produced until 1897, introduced a succession of powerful women protagonists including Cleopatra, Major Barbara, and Joan of Arc. Shaw's female characters are individuals, some sympathetic, some not. They generally triumph over men, whatever the circumstance or undertaking. Shaw does not make fun of women, and he never presents a woman as a ridiculous comic type. Nor are his young women stereotypically beautiful heroines or perfect Madonnas. Shaw also felt that the biological imperative makes women the natural aggressors. On the other hand, he seems to have feared the power that the sex drive could have over people, including himself.

The Man of Destiny (1896) is a slight play about the young Napoleon. *The Devil's Disciple* (1897) is a conventionally constructed play that is unconventional in its satirizing of romantic melodrama. It is set in the American Revolution and its hero, Dick Dudgeon, seemingly a ne'er-do-well, reveals his innate goodness by being willing to take the place of a condemned clergyman about to be hanged. The play is a comedy and so there is a last-minute reprieve. But, as this is a Shavian play, the intended sacrifice is not for love.

Caesar and Cleopatra (1898) gave Shaw an opportunity to attack "Bardolatry." He invited comparison to Shakespeare, believing himself the better, or at least the more moral dramatist. The play, in which Caesar is a committed pragmatist and Cleopatra is a spoiled child, serves as a delightful prequel to Shakespeare's *Antony and Cleopatra*.

Meanwhile Shaw was exhausting himself with writing plays, reviewing, and making speeches. In 1898 the forty-two-year-old playwright suffered a physical breakdown from overwork. Earlier Shaw had befriended an Anglo-Irish heiress, Charlotte Payne-Townshend. Charlotte, learning that Shaw was very ill, came to his mother's flat–where he still lived–and carried him away to her apartment where she brought in doctors who performed an operation that may have saved his life. None of Bernard and Charlotte's mutual friends, like the Webbs, dreamed that they would marry. But they did and were married for forty-five years, until Charlotte died in 1943. They had no children. Their first home was in London, but in 1906 they bought a country manor house, the former rectory of the Hertfordshire village of Ayot St. Lawrence, where they spent the rest of their long lives. Some felt it strange that the ardent socialist, supposedly a confirmed bachelor and given to ménage à trois relationships, would marry a very wealthy woman. The marriage apparently was celibate. Shaw's continuing flirtations with actresses were not sexually consummated.

You Never Can Tell (1899), a domestic comedy in which a hotel waiter at a seaside resort brings a divided family together again, followed *Caesar and Cleopatra*. *Captain Brassbound's Conversion* (1900) has Lady Cicely Waynflete, a typically strong Shavian woman, overcoming and taming the piratical Captain Brassbound. For many critics, *Man and Superman* (1903) is Shaw's masterpiece. Its hero, Jack Tanner, seems to be the most obvious spokesperson for the author in the Shavian cannon. The play argues that the life force in women makes them naturally dominant and so men, to compromise, must find enterprises to serve that are greater than their individual selves.

The next year Harley Granville–Barker and J. E. Vedrenne acquired the use of the historic Royal Court Theatre, and it was on that stage that Shaw built his great reputation as the leading dramatist in England, with eleven of his fifty-two plays premiering there. The first was *John Bull's Other Island* (1904), Shaw's brilliant treatise on the Irish question. *Major Barbara* (1905) is about a Salvation Army woman whose father is a munitions manufacturer. Barbara has to consider taking contributions from him, despite the antisocial source of the money, so that she can continue her good work. The moral dilemma is her challenge–one that is rather easily and oddly overcome.

The Doctor's Dilemma (1906) concerns a research physician who has discovered a cure for a deadly disease. He has produced only enough serum for a single dose and he has two patients whose life he could save. One is a hard–working slum physician. The other is a selfish, decadent, but very talented artist who just happens to have a beautiful, adoring, virtuous wife with whom the doctor is infatuated. Who gets the serum? *Misalliance* (1910) is about parent–children relationships in upper–class English society. When an airplane crashes into the greenhouse of the Tarlton estate, a Polish aviatrix brings turmoil to two respectable families.

Androcles and the Lion (1913) is Shaw's version of the fable about the slave who once removed a thorn from a lion's paw, and much later is recognized by the grateful beast who saves Androcles' life in the Roman Coliseum. A love affair between a Roman captain and a young Christian woman, as well as the internal struggle of a nonviolent Christian man trying not to use his strength against those who would kill him, enliven the play.

Pygmalion (1913) is one of Shaw's most popular plays. It is the story of the transformation of a working-class flower girl into a beautiful and charming woman who could pass for a duchess thanks to the efforts of a cantankerous and most un-romantic professor of phonetics.

When World War I broke out in 1914, Shaw spoke against it in *Common Sense about the War* (1914). As a result his plays disap-peared from the boards. His support for his native Ireland dur-ing and after the abortive Easter Rising in 1916 further distanced him from his London audience. A courageous production of *Arms and the Man* in 1919 began his rehabilitation. In 1920 a New York production of *Heartbreak House* brought back his American audience. That play is a dark comedy showing Shaw's pes-simism about the future of the post–World War I British upper class. It is also the play Shaw thought was his best.

Back to Methuselah (1922) is a series of five consecutive plays performed over several evenings. The epic drama covers all of human history and extols the value of longevity. It too opened in New York, but unlike *Heartbreak House*, it is seldom produced. After the brilliant *Saint Joan*–Shaw's version of the martyrdom of the testy saint–opened triumphantly in New York in 1923, the London audience could not wait to welcome him back. The award of the Nobel Prize for Literature in 1925 confirmed Shaw's international reputation as the greatest living English-language dramatist. George Bernard Shaw, the irreverent, icon-oclastic Irishman, is one of the giants of English literature.

Too True to Be Good (1932) makes fun of class prejudices, the British Army in the Middle East, and heroics. A burglar and his nurse accomplice convince a wealthy upper-class young woman who is ill with measles and mother love to run away with them, pretend she has been kidnapped, sell her jewels, and live it up in the Middle East on the money. The army is trying to fight bandits who do not exist and rescue the girl who is in no danger. At the behest of his preacher father, the burglar becomes a preacher too so that he will never be caught. And it turns out that an eccentric private–based on T. E. Lawrence (of Arabia)–brilliantly runs the entire Mesopotamian campaign while his colonel gets the credit and a knighthood.

The Millionairess (1936) is a play about the power of money and also its limitations. The title character, who thinks she can buy anything, is looking for a new husband. She is attracted to an altruistic Egyptian doctor who has very different values from her own. She tries to win him by a display of her business acumen put to use to assuage poverty.

Shaw continued to write plays until almost the last months of his life, but the productions of the 1940s did not prove popular. After falling and fracturing his thigh, George Bernard Shaw died at his home in Ayot St. Lawrence on November 2, 1950.

MAJOR   PLAYS

Widowers' Houses (1892)

Shaw's first play is an Ibsenite drama in which a young physician, Harry Trench, falls in love and becomes engaged to Blanche Sartorius, a women whose father's wealth comes from the ownership of slum housing where the poor are exploited. They are packed in tenements and with little choice but to pay the excessive rents. Symbolically, Trench is torn between his socialistic–or at least humane–ideals and the materialism of capitalism. Blanche refuses to renounce her father's wealth, and she ends the engagement. But Trench learns that some of his income is derived from the slums, and, cynically, he gives up principles and resigns himself to tainted wealth and the renewed affection of the bullying Blanche. Thus even in Shaw's first play, his antiromantic position is evident. The romantic impulse is a trap that diverts young people from clear–headed, intelligent reasoning and their best social instincts.

Mrs Warren's Profession (1894)

Although written in 1894, it was not until 1902 that Shaw could get Mrs Warren's Profession produced: the public was not ready to have prostitution discussed in terms other than that of it being an unmitigated social evil.

The play is set in a small town in Surrey where Vivie Warren lives, an intelligent, emancipated "New Woman" with a recent degree from Cambridge. She is expecting a visit from the mother she has not seen for many years, but who is reputed to be a very successful businesswoman and who has provided Vivie's education and all the luxuries she has enjoyed.

Vivie has a boyfriend, Frank Gardner, a pleasant but spoiled young man who is not too bright. He would like to marry Vivie partly because he knows her mother is wealthy and he has no intention of ever working for a living.

When Mrs. Warren arrives, she is accompanied by her "friend" and business partner Sir George Crofts. Crofts is a former lover who may be Vivie's father, although Mrs. Warren assures him that he is not. The reason that there is doubt about Vivie's paternity is that Mrs. Warren has been a prostitute. In the course of the play, Vivie learns that her mother not only was a prostitute but now owns a string of very profitable brothels on the Continent, with Crofts providing the political cover for the shady business. The middle-aged Crofts proposes marriage to Vivie, introducing a hint of possible incest into the play. Vivie refuses the arrogant and decadent Sir George.

Having learned of her mother's occupation, Vivie confronts her, demanding to know how she could have debased herself so, and how she could have profited from the exploitation of the bodies of young women like herself. Mrs. Warren defends her actions on the grounds that economic factors forced her into prostitution, and that, once in it, she was going to make a good thing of it as a madam instead of dying young from drugs or disease. Vivie is almost ready to understand and forgive her mother, but when she realizes that her mother has returned for the self-serving purpose of having Vivie take care of her in her old age, she says farewell to her mother. She will earn her own living and make her own way in life.

At the end both Vivie and Mrs. Warren seem hardened, the latter by the life she has led, and the former by the understanding of how hard life is for working-class women and how few and limited their choices are. Today *Mrs Warren's Profession* is a more popular play than it has ever been.

Arms and the Man (1894)

In *Arms and the Man*, Shaw makes fun of the idealism of love (not controversial) and war (very controversial in the heady days of the British Empire). The title comes from the opening line of the great epic poem of the Roman Empire, Virgil's *Aeneid*: "I sing of arms and the man."

In the play Shaw aims his satirical barbs at two targets: the romance of war and romantic love. "Arms" in the title could refer both to weapons and a woman's arms wrapped around the hero-soldier idealistically going off to his—meaningless, Shaw would say—death in battle. Dying "gloriously" in battle is of little use. The good soldier keeps himself alive.

The play is set in a small town in late-nineteenth-century Bulgaria, a nation at war with its stronger neighbor, Serbia. Unexpectedly, Bulgaria has just won a decisive battle. The curtain opens on the bedroom of Raina Petkoff, a beautiful young Bulgarian woman. Raina, in her nightgown, is thinking romantic thoughts about her lover, Sergius, a handsome cavalry officer who has led the charge that brought victory to the Bulgarians. Serb stragglers are running through the streets and Raina is warned to keep her lights off and away from her shuttered window.

Suddenly, a bedraggled Serb officer breaks in with a pistol drawn. The scene is charged with the possibilities of sex, rape, and violent death. However, Captain Bluntshli, who is a Swiss mercenary and not a Serb, is only interested in saving his skin and getting some sleep. His pistol is unloaded. He carries chocolates instead of cartridges. Raina quickly realizes she has the upper hand, even though she is angry when Bluntshli tells her that Sergius's "courageous" attack came about only because his horse had bolted toward the Serbian lines. Furthermore, Sergius and his troops would have been cut down by Bluntshli's machine gun battery but for the fact that they had been given the wrong ammunition. Raina cannot turn the poor wretch over to his executioners in the streets. She and her mother let him hide in her room, and the next day send him off in disguise with one of her father's coats.

A few months later, the war over, Sergius has returned and, disillusioned with army life, has resigned his commission. Bluntshli appears, intent on returning the coat. He is welcomed by Sergius and Raina's father, Major Petkoff, who have met him in the peace negotiations and who have heard only the general outline of his adventurous escape. Madam Petkoff urges him to depart, but Raina greets him warmly.

When Sergius gets a chance, he makes love to the servant

Louka, who informs him that she knows Raina had a man in her bedroom the night of the battle, for she had seen Bluntshli's pistol on an ottoman. Sergius, his honor compromised, demands to know who his rival is. Learning it is Bluntshli, he challenges the Swiss to a duel, but Raina intervenes and informs him of her romantic feelings for the stranger. Raina, who has seen Sergius with Louka and been disillusioned further, admits that she was playing the role of romantic lover and hero-worshiper with Sergius. Now he is happier off the pedestal and with a more earthy love. All are now fully aware that Raina was the girl in Bluntshli's story, while he tries to protect her by saying it was only a schoolgirl's game. But she is twenty-three years old, not seventeen as he thought. Delighted that at thirty-seven he is not too old for her, he offers marriage, a proposition that turns out to be very acceptable to the Petkoffs when they learn he is the heir of a hotel fortune in Switzerland.

Candida (1897)

Candida is the wife of a pompous and self-satisfied Christian socialist minister, the Reverend Morell. She is somewhat bored with motherhood and being a clergyman's wife until she is introduced to a young poet, Marchbanks, whom her husband has befriended. Marchbanks quickly falls in love with Candida, but Morell, always self-confident, takes it lightly. He does not see how his wife could be attracted to the callow youth. But she is. Marchbanks wants Candida to run away with him. Candida weighs the strengths and weaknesses of both men. Then, having decided that she would go with the weaker of the two males, she finds to her surprise that her husband and children need her much more than the poet does. Marchbanks has matured in the short time he has been infatuated; he has his artistic life ahead of him, and he has his idealism to sustain him, too. Understandably, actresses love the role of Candida.

Caesar and Cleopatra (1898)

Shaw's Caesar is an irreverent pragmatist who is quite willing to destroy the past and build the future on the ruins. He is past fifty, and although he does not know it, he has only four years to live. At the Sphinx, quite accidentally, he meets the charming, willful, cruel, frightened, immature Cleopatra, the sister of Ptolemy, the boy Pharoah, who is also her husband. She tells the old man who she is and that one day she will kill her brother and rule from the palace in Alexandria. She also informs him that the Roman Caesar is a barbarian who intends to eat her. Caesar starts to leave but the terrified girl begs him to take her with him.

Caesar and the unknowing girl arrive at the palace as the legions are approaching, and he advises her to sit on the throne and act like a queen. Her suspicious nurse, Ftatateeta, interferes and is put down by the commanding Caesar. Impressed, Cleopatra is willing to make him a king if he will stay by her, but first she wants to know how she can impress the terrible Caesar. Caesar instructs her in the appearance of authority. Dressed in her royal robes, she awaits the conqueror. The Romans enter, hail Caesar, and, understanding what has occurred, she falls into his arms.

Caesar confers with Britannus, a comic Briton slave who is Caesar's secretary and whose judgments reflect Shaw's view of middle-class Englishmen: easily shocked, supercilious, and quite sure that the British are the greatest people in the world. Under Caesar's tutelage, Cleopatra takes charge. She informs him that she loves a handsome Roman soldier who came to Egypt some time ago to save Egypt for her father. It is Mark Antony, and Caesar tells Cleopatra that it was he who sent him.

The Egyptians attack the Romans, and under siege, Caesar orders his ships burned and the seizing of the famous lighthouse. He learns that the great library of Alexandria is on fire, but he is indifferent because the records of the past hinder humankind with their myths and delusions. Only the future is important.

Meanwhile, the Egyptians have lifted the siege of the palace and are fighting the fire, which, it turns out, Caesar ordered set, so he could get himself and some of his troops to the safety of the lighthouse, which is on an island. Cleopatra wants to get to the safety of the lighthouse and so she has herself wrapped in a rug and delivered to Caesar as a "gift." When the Egyptians attack the lighthouse, Caesar jumps into the harbor and begins to swim. Cleopatra is thrown into the water after him and together they reach safety.

Five months later the Romans have won and Cleopatra rules from the palace. She has matured into a queen and a woman. At a banquet Caesar is thoughtful. He would like to leave corrupt, dangerous, and power-mad Rome behind and build a city for Cleopatra. But quickly he learns that she has taken bloody revenge on those who opposed her. Caesar denounces the folly of retribution. Disillusioned, he prepares to leave for Rome. He offers Britannus freedom, which is refused as the Briton would rather stay with Caesar. Cleopatra enters, beautiful and queenly, and Caesar promises to send her a gift from Rome: Mark Antony. A farewell kiss and Caesar departs after prophetically saying that he thinks they will never meet again.

In the character of Caesar, Shaw presented his idea of the mature, practical, intelligent leader—someone like Shaw. He is a doer not a dreamer. He has little vanity. He certainly has no sexual interest in Cleopatra. She is his pupil in statecraft. He desires to improve the world. For Shaw, the ideal leader's most important attribute is idealism.

Man and Superman (1903)

Man and Superman, produced in collaboration with Harley Granville-Barker before the latter assumed the artistic directorship of the Royal Court, has been considered by many critics as Shaw's finest play. It certainly made his reputation.

The subtitle of *Man and Superman* is *A Comedy and a Philosophy for Man and Superman*. It exposes Shaw's modus operandi as a dramatist. He gets an audience's attention with comedy so that they will listen to his economic, social, and political messages. In this play Shaw uses the Don Juan legend as a vehicle to depict the war of the sexes in England at the beginning of the twentieth century. A nearly middle–aged, wealthy, liberal English author named Jack Tanner represents Shaw. Tanner is good, moral, and chaste. Regardless, men can never win this war, for women have the life force in them and it both dominates them and makes them strong. Men of intelligence, on the other hand, need more to their lives than merely succumbing to nature's requirements. Ideally, men must prepare the world for the Nietzschean Supermen to come. They can best do that through avoiding marriage, but in the end Tanner gives in.

At the beginning of *Man and Superman*, Tanner and a man named Ramsden, who is a hypocrite, are to be joint guardians of the orphaned Ann Whitefield, a shrewd, contriving, but fascinating young woman. Ramsden objects to Tanner as a guardian because the latter has written a revolutionary book. Ann in fact had arranged the conditions of the will so that she can contrive to marry Tanner. When he realizes her plan, Tanner flees the country. After adventures with bandits, Tanner finally agrees to marry Ann. The life force cannot be denied after all.

Shaw constructed the four–act play so that it could be performed without its third act, Tanner's dream of hell in which he as Don Juan debates Satan while Ann as Doña Ana, the eternal female, looks on. That act, built on the characterizations in Mozart's *Don Giovanni*, is sometimes performed as a reading quartet under the title *Don Juan in Hell*.

John Bull's Other Island (1904)

At the request of William Butler Yeats, Shaw wrote *John Bull's Other Island* for the newly organized Irish Literary Theatre, later the Irish National Theatre Society based in the soon-to-be famous Abbey Theatre. But Yeats turned it down, perhaps because it was too provocative or simply because its large cast and several locations were too taxing for the impoverished company and their small theater. So Shaw gave the play to his friend Granville-Barker to initiate their long and brilliant collaboration at the Royal Court Theatre.

In depicting so-called English and Irish characteristics in *John Bull's Other Island,* Shaw inverted clichés. The play's chief Englishman, Tom Broadbent, is the one who is sentimental about Ireland, gushing over monastic ruins and admiring peasant life. The chief Irishman, the business partner in their engineering firm, Larry Doyle, is hardheaded, unsentimental, realistic, and very critical of Irish values and self-delusion. He thinks his native land and her people are backward.

Despite his sentimentality toward Ireland, Broadbent will make a profit from Ireland and win as his wife Nora, the woman who has been waiting for years for Doyle, her reluctant lover, to return and make her his bride. It is hilarious that the bumbling Broadbent will also become the member of Parliament in Westminster for the constituency of Rosscullen, Doyle's hometown. The Catholic small landowners of Rosscullen believe that they will get more out of an English MP than an Irish one. Doyle, with his education and business ability, should be the one to lead his family and former neighbors in the new century, but he is too indecisive, pessimistic, cynical, and skeptical concerning the abilities of his fellow Irishmen to take on the responsibility. The enterprising, ever-optimistic Englishman and presumably his countrymen will exploit the people and the land, and make their fortunes at Ireland's expense.

Shaw saw little point to the Irish independence movement when he was writing *John Bull's Other Island*. For him, Ireland could never be economically free from its larger and far wealthier neighbor across the sea. Destined to remain exploited by British capital as it had been for centuries, it did not seem to matter whether Ireland should or could be politically independent.

Although Larry Doyle is, like Shaw, an Irish self-exile in London, it is Peter Keegan, a defrocked Catholic priest, who speaks for Shaw's socialism. He is a visionary and an eccentric who talks to grasshoppers and cares about the poor. He is concerned about what he predicts will happen to the beautiful countryside when the English entrepreneurs begin to build their golf courses and put motor boats on the lakes, but Keegan does not have the political power to prevent the inevitable appropriation.

Shaw humorously condemns both the English and the Irish. Although all of Ireland was still part of the United Kingdom when Shaw wrote *John Bull's Other Island*, he foresaw the economic situation of postcolonial Ireland seventeen years before the establishment of the Irish Free State in 1921. Unfortunately, *John Bull's Other Island* is marred by Shaw's anti–Semitic characterizations in act 1.

Major Barbara (1905)

Barbara, the daughter of the rich munitions manufacturer Andrew Undershaft and his wife Lady Britomart, is a major in the Salvation Army. The primary subject of the play is salvation, not individual salvation in the religious sense, but the salvation of society through the reeducation of individuals. The Shavian paradox in *Major Barbara* is that since poverty causes people to sacrifice their morals, it is the source of sin, barring the poor from heaven. Thus money is the root of all virtue.

Barbara tries to convert her father from what she sees as a great evil, producing weapons of war. Undershaft wants capitalism to succeed, so he pays his workers well because poverty causes discontent and leads to revolution. Barbara comes to realize that it is money from rich capitalists that allows the Salvation Army to do its work. It seems a Faustian bargain and she gives up her ministry to the poor. The workers at her father's factory are well-fed, and since the hungry cannot be saved, she will save the well-fed.

Barbara's suitor Adolphus is a professor of Greek, but he is willing to bang a drum in the Salvation Army band to be near Barbara. Since Undershaft's son Stephen shows no aptitude for business, he disinherits the young man and makes the more intelligent Adolphus his heir. With Adolphus's brains and Barbara's zeal, Undershaft knows his business has a great future.

Throughout the play, Lady Britomart abhors what she sees as the immorality of her husband's occupation, but she never contemplates giving up the money capitalism provides. The delightfully absurd play leaves the audience both laughing and scratching their heads over Shaw's cleverly paradoxical message.

Pygmalion (1914)

The musical comedy version of Pygmalion, Alan J. Lerner and Frederick Loewe's My Fair Lady, has made the plot of this play Shaw's best known. Pygmalion is based on the legend of Pygmalion the sculptor who falls in love with an ivory statue he has made of a beautiful young woman. He prays to the gods to give it life, and when they do, he calls the living woman Galatea and marries her.

In Shaw's play, Professor Henry Higgins, an affluent, eccentric expert in phonetics, overhears a flower girl speaking with a strong cockney accent. As he "collects" her by taking phonetic notes, passersby think he is a policeman and try to defend her. One of them is Colonel Pickering, a retired officer in the British Indian army who is an authority on Indian languages and who has, coincidentally, come to London to seek out the famous professor. The men are delighted to meet each other, so Higgins gives the girl, whose name is Liza Doolittle, some money to end her complaints. Feeling flush, she takes a taxi home.

However, she has overheard the professor boast that he could teach her to speak so well that he could pass her off as a duchess in three months. The next day she arrives at his house by taxi and tries to hire him—with the money he gave her—to instruct her in how to sound upper class. Pickering bets Higgins that he cannot do it well enough to indeed pass her off as an aristocrat. Liza, somewhat fearfully for Higgins is a bully, buys into the scheme.

Liza's father, a dustman named Alfred Doolittle, arrives on the scene to see what has happened to his daughter. Seeing the men, he assumes wrongly that sex is behind the situation, but he is willing to be bought off with a five-pound banknote.

Higgins and Pickering train Liza for a period and then send her off on a test run to Higgins's mother's house where she also meets Mrs. Eynsford Hill, her daughter, and her son Freddie, who is attracted to the now well-scrubbed and tastefully dressed girl, who can only converse on two subjects: the weather and the health of relatives.

Then Higgins takes Liza to a ball, where she is mistaken for an aristocrat, and wins his bet. The men are deliriously happy and ignore Liza who grows furious. She flings his slippers at the demanding Higgins and goes to his mother's house. In the interim we learn that Mr. Doolittle has been left a large sum of money by an eccentric American to lecture on moral philosophy and is very unhappy in his new clothes and new respectability.

Higgins follows Liza, seeking her return, but it is clear that she will no longer be patronized by him. Instead she will either marry Freddy or teach other cockney flower girls to speak like duchesses. Eliza the cockney triumphs over the selfish, patriarchal, bullying professor.

It is clear that there is no romance between Liza and Higgins in Shaw's play. Shaw states in a postscript that Liza marries Freddie and they go into business together. The film industry and the American musical theater could not accept Shaw's antiromantic position and changed his ending.

Heartbreak House (1919)

Shaw starting working on this play as early as 1913. It took him six years to complete the drama. *Heartbreak House* is a pessimistic play written in a Chekhovian style. The debt to Chekhov is acknowledged in the subtitle: "A Fantasia in the Russian manner on English themes." The play is set in the Sussex home of Captain Shotover, an eccentric eighty-eight-year-old former sea captain and Shaw's spokesman in the play. He built Heartbreak House in the form of a ship, and it symbolizes England, a seafaring, island nation. Shotover is reputed to have sold his soul to the Devil in Zanzibar and married a witch in the West Indies. He is a heavy drinker of rum, which may or may not help him in his desire to attain the seventh degree of concentration, a kind of mystical meditation. Shotover's houseguests, like Chekhov's aristocrats, are for the most part idle people. His daughter Hesione Hushabye is a forty-four-year-old siren, and her busband Hector is a fifty-year-old roué and daydreamer who, in disguise, has been making love to Ellie Dunn, an attractive young singer engaged to Boss Mangan, a rapacious, middle-aged industrialist. He is killed near the end of the play by a bomb dropped from an attacking aircraft. Ellie is especially fond of the captain because of his apparent wisdom. The discussions, events, and discoveries of the play are primarily for her education.

Shotover's other daughter, Lady Ariadne Utterwood, age forty-two, is married to Sir Hastings Utterwood, a colonial administrator and British Empire builder. Lady Utterwood represents the aristocratic woman who spends her life overseas and is spoiled by servants and sycophants.

In the course of the play, Ellie is disillusioned with romance because of Hector's deceit and because it is revealed that Mangan is not wealthy himself but rather uses the money capitalists put up for investment. She is willing to marry the philosophical Shotover, but she is disillusioned by him too because his seventh degree of concentration turns out to be rum. Ellie is thus free to live her life as she wishes. The important thing is that despite the air raid Heartbreak House and England survive, although the future looks grim.

Saint Joan (1925)

The brilliant, continually revived *Saint Joan* offers several subjects for discussion including nationalism, individualism, and Protestantism as a reaction against the unchallenged spiritual authority of the Catholic Church and the secular power of the medieval state. Joan is an unusual saint, especially for depiction in drama, because she is a saint who fights back. She does so on the battlefield of course, but also in her witty and perspicacious responses to her inquisitors, rejoinders that are remarkably Shavian. Joan's "Protestantism" lies in her firm independence of thought and action, especially in regard to her insistence on directly following the orders of the spiritual voices that instruct her to act to save France. She needs no relay from heaven via an established church. Joan's nationalism is that she places the love of France above ecclesiastical authority.

Saint Joan's structure is that of a series of dramatized historical events. Jeanne d'Arc, a French peasant girl, lived from about 1412 to 1431. In 1429 she became a warrior in the Hundred Years War between France and England, helping to liberate part of her country from the rule of the English and their Burgundian allies. Her story of conquest, capture, betrayal, and martyrdom takes place in the last two years of her life, before she was condemned as a heretic by ecclesiastic authorities egged on by the English, and burned to death at the stake.

As the play begins, Joan comes to the French authorities with the news that God has sent her to obtain a horse, armor, and soldiers to accompany her to Charles, the dauphin of France, who will provide her with enough troops to raise the siege of Orleans and have him crowned king in Rheims Cathedral. Impressed by the girl's zeal, the authorities give her soldier's apparel and an escort to the court where Joan informs the timorous Prince Charles that she has been sent by God to drive the English back to their own country and make him king. Moved by Joan's passion, Charles consents to aid her.

Joan's antagonist, the English Duke of Warwick, is concerned about the victories Joan has achieved as leader of the revitalized French. He knows she must be destroyed somehow. Meanwhile Charles is crowned in Rheims although Joan is being undermined by jealous courtiers. She contemplates going home, but her voices want her to go on. She wants to take Paris, but Charles wants a peace treaty with the Burgundians. The archbishop of Rheims accuses her of disregarding God, but Joan follows the authority of her voices.

Finally Joan is captured by the Burgundians, sold to Warwick, and delivered by him to an ecclesiastic court in Rouen for trial on the charge of heresy. He wants her death and expects the Church will provide it. The clerics try to save her soul, but she will not confess to the charges against her, and she is condemned and executed by the soldiers, who lament her death

afterward and pray among her ashes. In the epilogue, an amusing, poignant, and cynical dreamlike sequence set in the bedroom of the now middle-aged Charles VII, a visitor from 1920
informs Joan that she is to be canonized. She offers to return to
earth, but her offer is declined because, as Joan's story illus-
trated, saints are much easier to deal with when dead than
when they are alive, involved, and interfering with the status
quo.

Additional Reading

Best, Charles A. *Bernard Shaw and the Art of Drama.* Urbana: University of
Illinois Press, 1973.

Ganz, Arthur. *George Bernard Shaw.* New York: Grove, 1983.

Gordon, David J. *Bernard Shaw and the Comic Divine.* New York: St. Martin's, 1990.

Holroyd, Michael. *Bernard Shaw.* New York: Random House, 1988.

Peters, Sally. *The Ascent of the Superman.* New Haven: Yale University
Press, 1996.

Shaw, Bernard. *Complete Plays with Prefaces.* New York: Dodd, Mead, 1975.

J. M. Barrie (1860–1937)

The stock in trade of J. M. Barrie's dramatic works is fantasy. For
him the theater was a place to be entertained. No Barrie fan
ever expected Ibsen-like realism or Shavian lectures in an in-
souciant Barrie play.

James Matthew Barrie was born in Kirriemuir, in the Scottish Lowlands. He was the son of a handloom weaver who was
an avid reader. Barrie's mother was the child of a stonemason.
When Barrie was six years old, his older brother, Mrs. Barrie's
favorite child, was killed in an accident, and Barrie set out to
replace his brother in his mother's heart. This is the source
of the lost children and the warm, loving mothers in Barrie's

work. Barrie was fortunate enough to receive a fine education including a master of arts from Edinburgh University in 1882.

Inspired by Robert Louis Stevenson and determined to make a career as a writer, Barrie worked as a journalist and a successful contributor of sketches and stories to journals. Then he left Scotland for London. A successful novel, *The Little Minister* (1891), confirmed his belief in himself as a professional writer. His first play, *Richard Savage* (1891), made little impression. In 1892 Barrie's farce *Walker* was more successful. By then earning enough to support a wife, Barrie married Mary Ansell, an actress, in 1904, but the marriage was reputed to be unconsummated.

In 1897 Barrie turned *The Little Minister* into a very successful melodrama. Now Barrie was recognized as a major British dramatist on both sides of the Atlantic. *Quality Street*, a sentimental comedy, was a success in 1892. The next year *The Admirable Crichton*, an unsentimental desert island tale of class reversal, proved to be Barrie's most highly regarded play except of course for the world's favorite children's play, *Peter Pan* (1904). That work that stemmed from the long relationship between Barrie and the five sons of Sylvia Llewelyn Davies, to whom he told many tales of fairies and pirates in the South Seas, which he had read about in Stevenson's novels. *Peter Pan* has had several musical adaptations. It was also turned into two films and a novel entitled *Peter and Wendy* (1906).

Other successful Barrie plays include *What Every Woman Knows* (1908), a satire on the importance of women to men's careers; *Dear Brutus* (1917), a play about getting second chances in life, and *Mary Rose* (1920), the story of the disappearance of a child bride who returns after many years but seems not to have aged. Barrie's later full-length plays were not commercially successful. Barrie wrote several successful one-act plays, the most famous being *The Old Lady Shows Her Medals* (1917).

In 1909, after fifteen years of marriage, Mary Barrie had an affair with another writer, Gilbert Cannan, and Barrie divorced her. When Sylvia Davies and her husband died, Barrie unofficially became the guardian of the five boys, providing for their upkeep and education.

Barrie received many awards in his lifetime, including several honorary degrees, a knighthood in 1913, and the Order of Merit in 1922. When he died in 1937 he was buried near his parents and brother in his hometown, Kirriemuir.

The world of Barrie's drama is one in which society's norms are reversed: the young are wiser than the old, and the lower classes are better equipped for survival than those above them. The protagonists in Barrie plays are always individuals trying to find themselves.

M A J O R   P L A Y S

The Admirable Crichton (1902)

In The Admirable Crichton, Barrie satirizes upper-class liberals who in their hearts are hypocrites. They profess a belief in equality but hold on tightly to their privileges. The Earl of Loam is one of those types. He demands that his servants have tea with him, even though they are uncomfortable doing so. Loam's butler, Crichton, is not a liberal and does not share his employer's views.

Loam and his three daughters go on a cruise. Only one maid and Crichton are willing to go with the lord. Other servants resign rather than do double or triple duty on the yacht, which ends up sinking in a Pacific storm. All reach an island except Loam, who was last seen trying to board the only lifeboat first. Initially class distinctions are kept up, but soon Chrichton, a natural leader, takes command.

Eventually Lord Loam washes ashore with some wreckage,

and his relatives demand that he exert his authority. All Loam does is lead the tiny band of aristocrats to another part of the tropic island, where they soon realize that they cannot survive without the enterprising Crichton. The former butler takes charge again, and he does not profess any phony liberalism. The former aristocrats must keep their lowly place and do the work he orders.

Oddly, the aristocrats become happy doing useful work for the first time in their lives. Loam is considered a harmless old man while Lady Mary, his attractive eldest daughter, falls in love with manly Crichton, who considers making her his consort, but when a ship appears, he realizes that he will soon be back in service.

At home all is as before, and Crichton is back in his place. Lady Mary still admires him, and, radicalized by the island experience, states that something may be wrong with English society. However, Crichton the butler will brook no criticism of the country he loves. Barrie offered a different ending in a revival with Crichton arguing against inequality, but the play was less funny that way, and he reverted to the "true to class" original ending in the published version of the text.

Peter Pan (1904)

Peter Pan is Barrie's children's classic, beloved by youngsters the world over, but it is also a play with great appeal to adults, invoking nostalgia for their own innocent days and memories of a loving mother. The drama vivifies a Freudian dreamworld of dangers: flying, wild savages, and fierce pirates. Peter Pan may have been in William Golding's mind when he wrote his darker version of boys' life in a world beyond the law of the father: Lord of the Flies (1954).

In the nursery of the Darling family one night when Nana the dog has the night off, Mrs. Darling is sleeping with her three children when she is awakened by the presence of a strange boy in the room. She screams just as Nana returns, and as the dog lunges the boy flees, leaving behind his shadow, which Mrs. Darling rolls up and stows in a drawer.

The next night Peter Pan, "the boy who would not grow up," returns with the fairy Tinker Bell and retrieves his shadow. He informs Wendy, the only daughter in the family, that he lives in Never Land with lost boys who once fell out of their prams. There the boys are in danger from Captain Hook, a pirate, who wants to get Peter for having torn off his arm and fed it to a crocodile, who is now looking for Hook in order to finish his dinner. Also in Never Land the boys are under the protection of a group of American Indians. Enchanted, Wendy and her two brothers fly with Peter and Tinker Bell to Never Land where Wendy becomes an excellent surrogate mother to the boys. But the jealous pirates want to kidnap her and make her their mother.

Worried about their parents, the Darlings ask Peter and the lost boys to go home with them. The boys are willing, but Peter insists on staying so he can remain a boy. The pirates, having learned of the intended return, seize all the children and tie Wendy to a mast. Peter now plans to get revenge on Hook and company who plan to have the boys walk the plank. Peter tricks the pirates into their deaths and causes Hook to throw himself overboard, where the croc has been waiting patiently.

Peter, Tinker Bell, Wendy, and all the boys fly back to the Darling domicile, but Peter chooses not to stay. The lost boys are adopted by the Darlings. Peter returns to persuade Wendy to go back to Never Land with him, but she refuses to leave her family again. She goes once a year to clean his house, but on each trip she sees Peter less clearly. Finally, Wendy can no longer make the trip, and Peter, who never understood that

Wendy would like him to think of her in other ways than as a mother, is left alone to play his pipes.

What Every Woman Knows (1908)

More Shavian in its realism than any other Barrie play, *What Every Woman Knows* is a social satire exploring the theme that a woman is always behind the success or failure of a man.

A Scottish family, the Wylies, are successful business people, headed by Alick the father and nurtured by Maggie, his plain daughter, age twenty-seven and apparently destined for spinsterhood. Her brothers James and David want to help her find a husband. An opportunity arrives when the brothers apprehend a burglar who turns out to be John Shand, a divinity student neighbor who broke into their house to read because he was too poor to buy the necessary books.

David offers to pay for John's education if he will promise to marry Maggie in five years provided she accepts him. John agrees. The agreed-upon period having passed and then some, we learn that John has abandoned his religious studies and is standing for a seat in parliament. Maggie agrees to wait until the election is over. John wins, but now he is pursued by attractive women. Maggie offers to release him from his bond, but John, being a man of his word, marries Maggie, who helps him in his career by writing his speeches. Soon, however, John grows tired of his plain wife and is enamored of the beautiful Lady Sybil.

John informs Maggie and her brothers that he is in love with Lady Sybil and would give up everything for her. The brothers remind John that to do so would destroy his political career. Maggie suggests that John go away with Sybil for a few weeks to write an important speech with Sybil's help while she keeps the affair a secret.

Upon his return, John learns from his political mentor that

the new speech is a disappointment, but Maggie saves the situation by informing the mentor that John has written another and better speech that she has typed. Meanwhile, Lady Sybil has grown bored with John and ended the affair. John is complimented on the speech that Maggie has written. She informs him that every important man who has climbed high thinks that he has achieved the heights alone, but every wife knows better. They laugh and are reconciled.

The triumph of the good wife over the siren made the moralistic, sentimental, but also humorous play a favorite for actresses and audiences from the Edwardian period through the 1930s.

Dear Brutus (1917)

Written in the dark days of World War I, *Dear Brutus* is a fantasy based on Shakespeare's *A Midsummer Night's Dream*. On Midsummer Eve in a country house owned by Lob, a group of women guests, having learned that Matey the butler had stolen jewelry from one of them, promise not to inform on him if he tells them why they have been invited to the dinner party. He cannot tell them, but they do learn that their host is ageless and that his name is another name for Puck. Matey warns them not to stray beyond the garden into the woods, but they cannot see any woods.

When woods magically appears in the place of the garden and all the guests, female and male, decide to venture into them, where it turns out that on Midsummer Eve people have a second chance at finding happiness in relationships old or new. They may also come to a better understanding of themselves. When they return to reality at dawn, they have learned that they themselves have made their destinies, not fate. Social discord is resolved and general forgiveness and understanding ensue. Lob, thanked for making all this possible, goes back to

tending the flowers in the garden and, presumably, to wait for
the next Midsummer Eve.

Additional Reading

Barrie, J. M. *The Plays of J. M. Barrie, in One Volume.* New York: Scribners,
1929.

Dunbar, Janet. *J. M. Barrie: The Man behind the Image.* Boston: Houghton
Mifflin, 1970.

John Galsworthy (1867–1933)

Like George Bernard Shaw, John Galsworthy was awarded the
Nobel Prize for Literature (1932). He was one of the best known
and most influential British authors in the first half of the
twentieth century. Famous for his enormously popular epic ac-
count of three generations of an upper–middle–class English
family, *The Forsyte Saga* (1906–1921), Galsworthy was also one of
the leading dramatists of his time. He was a playwright of conscience, writing serious plays about serious societal problems
such as labor–management struggles, class conflict, an unfair
justice system that privileged the rich and penalized the poor,
anti–Semitism, and other issues. His dramatic style followed the
naturalism of Ibsen. Galsworthy wrote twenty–two full–length
plays and many one–act plays.

John Galsworthy was born in Kingston Hill, Surrey. His father, John Galsworthy, was a wealthy solicitor and company director, and his mother, the former Blanche Barleet, was the
daughter of a wealthy manufacturer. He had a privileged childhood and youth. After Harrow he went to Oxford where he
took a second–class degree in law and heavily pursued sports.
His father wanted his son to become a barrister and to succeed
him in business. Galsworthy was called to the bar in 1890, but,
to his father's disappointment, he never actually presented a

case to a judge. Instead Galsworthy began to travel around the world. Fatefully, sailing from Australia in 1892, he met and became friends with a merchant marine officer named Joseph Conrad, and years later, when Galsworthy began to write seriously, Conrad, then a successful author, aided his friend.

In 1891, before leaving on his travels, Galsworthy attended the wedding celebration for his cousin Arthur Galsworthy and Ada Pearson Cooper. The marriage was an unhappy one from the start. Four years later John Galsworthy fell in love with Ada and they began a love affair. After seven years, and upon the death of the senior John Galsworthy, Ada formally left her husband. Ada was divorced and the couple at last were able to marry in 1907. Marital strife, abused wives, divorces, and second chances at love were staples of Galsworthy's fiction and plays.

Early in the love affair, Ada suggested to John–who had no occupation except Ada–that he take up writing during the many weeks they had to be apart. By the time they were married, Galsworthy had published five novels and two plays. *A Man of Property* (1906), a novel, was a great success. It became the initial installment of *The Forsyte Saga*. Galsworthy's first produced play, *The Silver Box* (1906), dramatized the inequities of the English justice system. The play was a hit and Galsworthy, a prolific writer, threw a significant part of his energies into the theater. Like Shaw, he saw the stage as a platform for a debate on political reform and social justice.

Other stage successes included *Strife* (1909), in which a union leader and a manufacturer battle without concern for those they serve; *Justice* (1910), which caused Winston Churchill, the Liberal Home Secretary, to consult with Galsworthy about prison reform; *The Eldest Son* (1912), which showed that there are different rules for different classes; *The Skin Game* (1920), which portrays an archetypal, unreasonable feud between two rich families; and *Loyalties* (1922), in which a Jew seeking justice finds that society is on the side of the gentile scoundrel who robbed him.

The BBC literary television series *The Forsyte Saga* (1967) revolutionized the industry, brought millions of new readers to Galsworthy's work, and resulted in frequent revivals of his plays.

MAJOR PLAYS

The Silver Box (1906)

In *The Silver Box*, two men steal. On a whim Jack Barthwick, the son of a wealthy member of Parliament, steals a handbag with a purse in it from a prostitute with whom he has spent an evening. Jim Jones, the unemployed husband of the elder Barthwick's charwoman, steals a silver cigarette box and the once-stolen purse from the Barthwick residence. The prostitute threatens prosecution, and the elder Barthwick tries to bribe her off to keep knowledge of the affair out of the press. He also suspects the charwoman of theft. Mrs. Jones is very frightened.

The case goes on trial, and in a police court it is soon proved who really stole the box. Jones goes to jail while Jack, counseled by expensive attorneys, gets off scot free. The liberalism of the senior Barthwick is shown to be superficial when his self-interests are threatened. When, having lost her job at the end of the play, Mrs. Jones turns to her former employer in supplication, he slinks away, his hypocrisy revealed. The innocent charwomen suffers the most. Jim Jones utters the moral of the play: "Call this justice? What about 'im? E got drunk. E took the purse ... but ... its is money got im off–*Justice?*'"

With the *Silver Box*, Galsworthy hit on a technique that he would use throughout his playwriting career, that of dramatic contrast. Characters and situations are presented in simple and distinct pairs: in this play a rich and a poor son, a rich and a poor parent, a wealthy home and a poor one. In the way of naturalism, the audience makes the comparisons and does the judging. Galsworthy avoids melodrama and propaganda.

Strife (1909)

Strife is one of the first British dramas to depict the growing conflict in British society between labor and capital that led to the great strike of 1911 and the General Strike of 1926. Two antagonists, firebrand David Roberts, a union leader, and old, obstinate John Anthony, chairman of the board of the Trenartha Tin Plate Works, fall like hubristic Greek tragic heroes because of the backsliding and disaffection of their followers, whom they have outdistanced in their anger and fury. In the end the audience is stunned by the conflict, yet it admires both men for their principles and even comes to sympathize with the fallen leaders. Indeed, the combatants come to respect each other for their strength and the passion of their positions.

The play's action covers only a few hours. The company board meets to try to bring the strike to an end. Neither Anthony nor Roberts will compromise let alone give in. Separate meetings by the workers and the owners show Galsworthy's structural use of balanced parallelism. At the end of the play, a reasonable compromise is reached at the cost of the power of the unbending enemies, but not before there is suffering and death. Ultimately, *Strife* is more about the archetypal struggle of aggressively blind men to win the dangerous game of pride they love to play than it is about a confrontation between labor and management. Galsworthy implied that extremism wreaks havoc with a society that should be based on tolerance and good will.

Justice (1910)

Galsworthy abhorred incarceration. With *Justice* he built a platform—in the manner of Shaw—to denounce the physical degradation, the mental torture, and the moral disintegration that long imprisonment creates. The play's title is ironic. Formal justice is not just; it is a machine that rolls out a terrible product.

In *Justice*, a young man named Falder is discovered to have forged a check. He intended to use the money to go abroad with the woman he loves, a married woman whose husband has mistreated her (Galsworthy's perennial situation). Refusing to be merciful, his employer turns him in to the authorities, and justice begins its grinding motion. Falder's defense attorney pleads for some understanding of how a gentle but weak man, emotionally distressed by the brutal treatment of the woman he loves, could act as he did. Alas, judge and jury are prejudiced because Falder's lover is a married woman even though adultery has not taken place. Falder is found guilty of forgery and sentenced to three years imprisonment.

In prison Falder spends three months in the requisite solitary confinement. The loneliness and boredom nearly drive him mad. The prisoner is driven to flinging himself on the cell door and beating on it with his fists. When finally released, he tries to get his job back, but his hard-hearted former employer has little pity for a "gaol-bird" and will only give Falder a chance if he gives up his lover, who has separated from her husband. He cannot do that. She is the only person who cares for him. So he forges a reference to get a new position. About to be arrested again, the thought of prison hell drives him to jump to his death over a flight of stairs. As in *The Silver Box*, *Justice* shows how merciless and counterproductive the rigid justice system is, and how individuals struggle futilely when trapped in it.

Loyalties (1922)

In *Loyalties* Galsworthy decries the British upper-class tendency to close ranks against "others'" in society and remain loyal to their own even when their own have done wrong.

Ferdinand De Levis, a wealthy nouveau-riche Jew, is forced to fight alone against racial prejudice when he is robbed of a thousand pounds while spending a weekend with upper-class "friends." He believes that Captain Ronald Dancy, who previously had given De Levis a racehorse with which the latter made money, has broken into De Levis's room and taken the money. De Levis accuses Dancy, and all society rises to support the officer. They cut De Levis, ostracize him, and drive him out of his club.

Dancy sues De Levis for defamation of character after challenging him to a duel that De Levis refuses. An investigation reveals that Dancy indeed stole the money in order to pay off a former mistress. The court finds for De Levis, who informs his antagonist that he need not pay back the money nor pay the court costs. Finally disgraced, Dancy takes his own life with a shot through the heart.

The world-wise De Levis seeks justice. He knows he is only tolerated for his money, but he will not let society insult him and enjoy his money too. Ranged against De Levis is the personal loyalty to Dancy of "gentlemen" who cannot consider a Jew to be one of their number and the loyalty of family members to a loved one even when that person has committed a crime. De Levis's loyalty to his coreligionists is portrayed as honorable. It more than balances the specious loyalty of a class to itself. There is a Shakespearean echo in *Loyalties*: De

Levis is a Shylock sans meanness. Dancy is an Antonio without honor.

Additional Reading

Coates, R. H. *John Galsworthy as a Dramatic Artist.* London: Duckworth, 1926.

Dupont, V. *John Galsworthy: The Dramatic Artist.* Paris: Didier, 1942.

Dupré, Catherine. *John Galsworthy.* New York: Coward, McCann & Geoghegan, 1976.

Galsworthy, John. *The Manaton Edition of the Works of John Galsworthy.* London: Heinemann, 1923–1936.

Sternlicht, Sanford. *John Galsworthy.* Boston: G. K. Hall, 1987.

W. Somerset Maugham (1874–1965)

In 1908 W. Somerset Maugham had four plays running simultaneously in London. Prior to that year the novelist, short story writer, and dramatist had been mildly successful, but now he had managed, in a masterful way, to combine comedy and the well-made play into productions that delighted the audiences of the time. He also had learned from Wilde and Shaw that the best way to get a message across to an unsuspecting British audience was to wrap it in laughs. But Maugham consciously rejected Shaw's comedy of ideas that could lead to reform, because he was basically too pessimistic about humankind to believe it could change.

William Somerset Maugham was born in Paris. French was his first language. His father was a legal advisor to the British embassy in the French capital. His mother died when Maugham was eight years old, and his father died when Maugham was ten. A middle-aged maiden aunt and her vicar brother raised the boy in Whitstable, located near Canterbury. His was not a happy childhood and he became a lifelong stammerer.

Maugham was educated at Kings School, Canterbury, and at Heidelberg University in Germany where he became fluent in German. Having decided on a medical career, Maugham trained as a physician at St. Thomas's Hospital, London. After qualifying in 1897, his experience as a medical student and a young doctor to the poor in London's East End led him to writing, and early modest successes permitted Maugham to give up medicine for a career as a professional writer.

In 1911 Maugham met Syrie Bernardo Wellcome and she soon became his mistress. Syrie later became a well-known interior decorator. They had one child, Liz, born in 1915, and the couple married the next year. The marriage was unusual. Maugham's sexuality was ambiguous, but primarily homosexual, and so the couple spent relatively little time together. They were divorced in 1928 after a bitter feud.

In 1914 Maugham joined an ambulance unit for service in France in World War I. There he met Gerald Haxton, eighteen years his junior, who became his secretary and lover. They traveled much of the world together. In 1926 Maugham bought the Villa Mauresque at Cap Ferrat on the French Rivera, where he entertained his lovers and where he was often visited by the rich and famous of his time. He resided at his villa for the remainder of his life. W. Somerset Maugham was awarded many honors, British and French, in his long lifetime.

Maugham's first dramatic success was *Lady Frederick* (1907), a comedy in which a woman is beset with marriage proposals. Successful comedies of manners include *Our Betters* (1917), in which Maugham began a long retreat from war to the drawing room in showing how viciously corrupt society can be, and how it is riddled with adultery; *Home and Beauty* (1919), a farce in which a woman prefers a World War I black market operator to two war heroes who also court her; *The Circle* (1921), Maugham's most frequently revived play; *East of Suez* (1922), a product of

Maugham's travels in the Orient in which he recreates the atmosphere of the East as seen through British eyes; and *The Constant Wife* (1926), in which a long-suffering wife breaks out and achieves independence so that she can elope to Italy with her lover. Maugham also wrote an antiwar play during the 1930s peace movement: *For Services Rendered* (1932). All in all, Maugham wrote some thirty full-length plays.

The most important and famous of Maugham's nondramatic works are the novels *Of Human Bondage* (1915), *The Moon and Sixpence* (1919), *Cakes and Ale* (1930), and *The Razor's Edge* (1944), and also the often dramatized short story "Rain" (1921).

M A J O R   P L A Y

The Circle (1921)

In *The Circle*, Maugham savages societal hypocrisy while stating that the young must be served. Elizabeth, a young society wife, considers running off with her lover despite the ostracism that she would face. Her husband, Arnold Champion-Cheney, MP, is a rising politician, the son of another politician who could have been prime minister but for the fact that he divorced Arnold's mother, Lady Kitty, after she left him for Lord Porteus. Elizabeth's lover is a young man working as a planter in Malaya and thus immune to hypocritical class values of upper-class British society.

Arnold's father, Clive Champion-Cheney, has been buying sex from young mistresses since the departure of his wife, and he concocts a scheme to keep his daughter-in-law married and save his son's career. Arnold tries to trap his wife by seemingly generously offering her a divorce and even an allowance if she chooses to leave the marriage, thus putting her under an obligation unacceptable to the young woman with integrity. Furthermore, the bored, old adulterers Lady Kitty and Lord

Porteus are paraded in to show the sorry results of their elope-
ment, illustrating that passion is fleeting and that a life spent in
the pursuit of pleasure is a sad one, surely not worth giving up
a high position in society.

Generational events come full circle, but the wife realizes
that the more moral alternative to sacrificing love for an un-
loved husband's career and social position is running away
with the man she loves. Audiences were deeply shocked at a
play that they saw favoring adultery, indeed implying that
abandoning an unsatisfactory marriage could be more moral
than staying in one.

Additional Reading

Barnes, Ronald Edgar, Jr. *The Dramatic Comedy of Somerset Maugham.* The
    Hague: Mouton, 1968.
Calder, Robert. *Willie: The Life of Somerset Maugham.* London: Heinemann,
    1989.
Maugham, W. Somerset. *Collected Plays.* London: Heinemann, 1952.
Morgan, Ted. *Maugham.* New York: Simon and Schuster, 1980.

Harley Granville-Barker (1877–1946)

Harley Granville-Barker was a master of naturalistic drama as
an author, director, and actor. He has been called Britain's first
modern theater director. British theater is forever in his debt
because his collaboration with Shaw and John E. Vedrenne at
the Royal Court helped create a theater of ideas and intellectual
content that strove to improve society by making it aware of
the significant social problems of the early years of the twentieth century.

Granville-Barker was born in Kensington, London, in 1877.
After a few years of private instruction, he joined a regional
stock company at age thirteen. Twelve years later, he was act-

ing professionally on the London stage. In 1906 Granville–Barker married the actress Lillah McCarthy. During World War I, Granville–Barker first served with the Red Cross and then joined British military intelligence. As the war came to a close, he divorced Lillah and married Helen Gates, an American writer who had him give up his career in theater production. Instead he became a theater scholar, critic, and theorist.

Granville–Barker's most significant contribution to drama theory is his *Prefaces to Shakespeare* (1923–1937). This work led to his appointment to the Clark Lectureship at Trinity College, Cambridge, in 1930, and he became Romanes Lecturer at Oxford in 1937. Later that year he was appointed the director of the British institute in Paris. When World War II began, Granville–Barker left France for the United States to serve as a visiting professor at Yale and Harvard. After the war he returned to Britain in poor health and then moved to Paris where he died in 1946. Granville–Barker received several honorary degrees.

Successful Granville–Barker plays include *The Voysey Inheritance* (1905), a play in which a son inherits his father's business only to find that his father had misused clients' money, and in which a "New Woman" actually proposes marriage to a man; *Waste* (1907), a tragedy of illicit love, abortion, and suicide, in which the protagonist, a powerful politician, advocates the disestablishment of the Church of England so that money can flow to a system of free secular education; and *Madras House* (1910), a comedy depicting how a woman's class determines how well she is treated.

MAJOR PLAY

Madras House (1910)

The fashion designer Constantine Madras is estranged from his wife. He has been living in the East and has become a Muslim. He now has returned to sell off the business. His son Philip has been running the fashion house in his father's absence. Philip wants to do more. In fact he wants to help humanity by becoming a city councilor. Paradoxically, the fashion house makes money by exploiting sexuality, getting women to dress like whores, while requiring the strictest morality from the women who work there. The business rules force the women employed by the fashion house to live under stringent moral supervision. If they are married, they must conceal the fact or lose their jobs. The world of the play is a hypocritical one. One saleswoman is pregnant and refuses to reveal the name of the father who, it turns out, is Constantine.

Constantine attacks the Protestant ethic in the fashion business that depersonalizes women and, in order to sell garments, treats them as economic units. Constantine could be a character by Shaw, for he is also a practicing polygamist.

His wife Amelia visits the home of her strong-willed sister Katherine and her six daughters, all of whom tote Bibles around, and all of whom are moving toward middle age and spinsterhood. They contrast with the saleswomen in the fashion house and the models, all of whom, despite restrictions, have a fuller life. Although little is resolved and the audience is left to contemplate competing values, *Madras House* is striking because it was one of the first feminist plays on the modern British stage.

Additional Reading

Granville–Barker, Harley. *Collected Plays*. London: Sedgwick and Jackson, 1937.

———. *The Use of Drama*. Princeton: Princeton University Press, 1946.

Frederick Lonsdale (1881–1954)

Frederick Lonsdale was a master of both light comedy and high comedy like his contemporary, W. Somerset Maugham. Lonsdale's plots are slight, but he surprises audiences while keeping them guessing about resolution. Lonsdale also wrote librettos and lyrics for several successful musical comedies.

Lonsdale was born Lionel Frederick Leonard on the island of Jersey. His father was a shopkeeper who sold tobacco. He joined the army at the age of eighteen and later went to sea as a merchant seaman. In Canada he worked on a farm. His career as a dramatist began with the fabulous success of having three plays simultaneously on the boards in the West End during the 1908–1909 season.

Lonsdale was a popular playwright for forty-two years. His most esteemed plays are *Aren't We All* (1923), a domestic comedy in which a wife returns from Egypt only to find her husband in the arms of another woman; his defense is the information that she returned because she, too, had been tempted by adultery. In *The Last of Mrs Cheney* (1925), a shady lady pretending to be an Australian is, in fact, part of a gang of jewel thieves preparing to rob her hostess. *On Approval* (1926), a play about a trial "marriage" between a haughty widow and an easy-going suitor, culminates in a battle royal among four rude people. Lonsdale's final play, *The Way Things Go* (1950), was produced only four years before his death.

Additional Reading
Donaldson, Frances. *Freddy Lonsdale.* London: Heinemann, 1957.

D. H. Lawrence (1885–1930)

D. H. Lawrence is of course one of the great modern novelists, and *Sons and Lovers* (1913), *The Rainbow* (1915), and *Women in Love* (1920) are a part of the canon of Western literature. But Lawrence was also a playwright. Although Lawrence was an innovator as a modern novelist, he followed Shaw and Galsworthy in his projections of society onto the stage. But Lawrence differed from his contemporaries in that he was less interested in illustrating society's problems than was Galsworthy, and less interested in offering solutions to those problems than was Shaw. Lawrence focused on the relationships between characters and the passions that drove them on.

David Herbert Lawrence was born in Eastwood, Nottinghamshire, a mining village. His father was a poorly educated coal miner and his mother was a well-educated and refined school teacher. She had a dominant personality and thus the couple did not get along very well. Lawrence was deeply attached to his mother. He won a scholarship to Nottingham High School, and after graduation he worked briefly as a clerk before obtaining a teaching position. He also studied at the University of Nottingham.

After several love affairs, Lawrence met Frieda von Richthofen Weekley, the German-born wife of a professor at the University of Nottingham. They fell passionately in love, and she deserted her husband and children to be with Lawrence. Divorce and marriage followed in 1914. Frieda was able to see her children again only rarely. Lawrence had tuberculosis, a fact he refused to accept, but the couple traveled much of the world seeking relief from the condition that eventually killed him.

Lawrence wrote eight plays, but only two came to the boards while he was alive. The reasons for this were the scandal over his marriage, the fact that his novels were attacked or banned because of their sexual content, and the short, peripatetic life he lived.

Lawrence's most important plays are an autobiographical trilogy about Nottingham life and the war between the sexes. *A Collier's Friday Night* (1909, first staged in 1968) shows how the patterns of behavior between men and women are passed on from generation to generation, as well as the impact of alcoholism on family life. *The Widowing of Mrs Holroyd* (1911, first staged in 1926) is a play about a wife who withholds her love and breaks her husband's will to live. And *The Daughter-in-Law* (1912, first staged in 1967), shows how a woman's cultural pretensions prove destructive to her working–class husband. All three plays are informed by Lawrence's misogynistic beliefs.

Additional Reading

Kermode, Frank. *D. H. Lawrence*. New York: Viking, 1973.

Lawrence, D. H. *The Complete Plays of D. H. Lawrence.* New York: Viking, 1973.

Leavis, F. R. *D. H. Lawrence*. 1930. Reprint, New York: Haskell House, 1972.

Ben Travers (1886–1980)

Like Frederick Lonsdale, Ben Travers mastered audience-pleasing light comedy and farce, the staples of British theater in the first half of the twentieth century. Travers was born in London and educated at Charterhouse, a top–rung public school. He served his country with distinction in the Royal Air Force in World War I and World War II.

Travers's nine Aldwych farces–so called because they were performed at the Aldwych Theatre–had the kind of impact on the British audiences of his day that Alan Ayckbourn's plays have today. The best regarded of them are *A Cuckoo in the Nest* (1925), in which a man's major concern is saving his respectability after having to spend an innocent night in a hotel room with a married woman; *Rookery Nook* (1926), where the hero tries to get proper clothes on a girl thrown out of her home by her violent father; *Thark* (1927) in which a lugubrious butler named Death nearly scares everyone else to death; and *Plunder*

(1928), in which jewel thieves steal goods that turn out to the property of one of them.

The long-lived and very productive dramatist's last play was *The Bed before Yesterday* (1975). Travers wisely set it in the 1930s, the era he knew best. In the play, a widow who has not had a satisfactory sex life comes to know the pleasures of sex with the help of the younger generation of liberated women. It was a hit when he was ninety years old.

Travers's comedies played off against a rigid and often hypocritical British society. They satirized social climbers, bumbling males, hefty matrons, and beset lovers. Married men in trouble provide sexual titillation even though they never do succeed in seduction. Travers's situations are sexy, but because his men strike out, morality triumphs in the end.

Additional Reading
Travers, Ben. *Vale of Laughter: An Autobiography.* London: G. Bies, 1957.

8

Between the Wars

The Jazz Age and the Depression

Clemence Dane (1888–1965)

Playwright and novelist Clemence Dane made her reputation in the theater with *A Bill of Divorcement* (1921), a play in part about the social upheaval in the aftermath of the cataclysm of World War I. Dane deserves more of a reputation than posterity has given her. She liked to write biographical plays about literary figures such as *Will Shakespeare* (1921), a drama in blank verse, and *Wild Decembers* (1932), about the Brontës. Her last hit was *Eighty in the Shade* (1958). Dane was born Winifred Ashton in London. She studied at the Slade School of Art for three years and in Dresden. From 1913 to 1918 she worked as an actress under the name Diana Cortis and, deciding to pursue a career as a writer, adopted the pen name Clemence Dane from the famous London church St. Clemens Danes built by Christopher Wren in 1680. In 1953 Dane was made a Commander, Order of the British Empire.

MAJOR PLAY

A Bill of Divorcement (1921)

Dane built her plot around the changes in British divorce laws brought about in part by the agitation of the women's suffrage movement. She has two generations debate the moral responsibilities that come with marriage, childbearing, and divorce. An independent young woman, Sydney Fairfield, a flapper, in the exuberance that followed World War I only wants to have a good time and then marry and settle down. She is not interested in a career. When Sydney's father comes out of the insane asylum where he has been held since returning from the war, she urges her mother to carry out her plan to divorce and remarry.

As Sydney is convinced that her father is congenitally mad, she decides to break off with her fiancé and care for her father. She is a student of eugenics as is her boyfriend, Kit. They would not want to risk bringing a mentally ill child into the world, for Sydney fears that she may have inherited her father's disease. Her mother is appalled that her young, unmarried daughter is so knowledgeable about sex and birth, but Sydney knows she must take moral responsibility for her life. She chooses a career after all, as marriage is out of the question for her.

Additional Reading
Dane, Clemence. *The Collected Plays of Clemence Dane.* London: Heinemann, 1961.

T. S. Eliot (1888–1965)

Born in St. Louis, Missouri, of a distinguished family originally from New England, Thomas Stearns Eliot lived most of his professional life in Britain where he rose to eminence as one of the greatest and most influential poets of the twentieth century. As an essayist and critic, Eliot exerted significant power over British and American poetry for a half century. Eliot wrote only eight plays, but the seriousness of his drama and his clear objective of adding a spiritual dimension to contemporary society made his work in the theater a counterbalance to the large number of banal plays on the boards in Britain and America from the post–World War I period through the years immediately after World War II. Eliot led the revival of the verse play that culminated in the work of Christopher Fry in the post–World War II period.

T. S. Eliot was educated at Harvard where he received a bachelor of arts and a master of arts in philosophy in four years. A year in Paris to study French literature followed. He continued his studies in philosophy at Merton College, Oxford. Eliot decided to remain in England and write poetry while teaching at a school in London. He later worked in Lloyds Bank. In 1914 Eliot met Ezra Pound who introduced Eliot to the writer's world and helped him get his poems published.

Eliot married Vivienne Haigh–Wood in 1915, just as his first great poem, "The Love Song of J. Alfred Prufrock," was published. The marriage was troubled early on although the couple lived together for almost two decades. They separated in 1933 following which Vivienne was committed to a mental institution where she remained until she died in 1947.

In 1922 Eliot's long and most distinguished poem, *The Waste Land,* appeared. With it, Eliot became the voice of his disillusioned and despairing generation. In 1925 Eliot began working as a literary editor for a publishing house that later became Faber and Faber. Eventually, he became a director of the company. In 1927 Eliot joined the Anglican Church and became a British subject. Continuing to write distinguished poetry and criticism, Eliot became the literary lion of his time.

In the 1930s Eliot decided to revive poetic drama on the commercial stage. The first significant result was *Murder in the Cathedral* (1935), a play about Christian martyrdom that is reminiscent of medieval drama and Greek tragedy. Eliot's next play was *The Family Reunion* (1939), a country house mystery overlaid

with elements from the *Oresteia* of Aeschylus. Three dark comedies followed. *The Cocktail Party* (1949), based on Euripides's *Alces-
tis*, is a satire on the vacuity of middle-class life. *The Confidential
Clerk* (1953) is a farce about the precariousness of identity. *The
Elder Statesman* (1958) finds Eliot at last turning to Ibsen-like
realism.

In 1948 Eliot received the Nobel Prize for Literature and the
Order of Merit. He married once more in 1957 to Valerie
Fletcher.

MAJOR   PLAYS

Murder in the Cathedral (1935)

Written for the Canterbury Festival of 1935, *Murder in the
Cathedral* is T. S. Eliot's most performed play. In it, a mostly
poetic drama about the assassination of Archbishop Thomas
Becket at Canterbury Cathedral in 1170, Eliot explores the conflict between church and state in the Middle Ages and the suffering that a man of conscience had to endure to protect the
authority of the church he served.

The tempters, in the form of four determined knights, come
to convince Thomas to obey the orders of his former friend and
patron, King Henry II. To avoid being killed by the knights,
Becket must compromise with the temporal power and he
could become Chancellor of England once more. Or he could
lead a revolt against the king, and ecclesiastical power could
reign supreme. The last temptation is that of eternal glory
through martyrdom and sainthood.

The murderous knights come to Canterbury and charge
Becket with treason and order him to leave the country, but he
is determined never to leave England again. The knights murder him in the cathedral and make their excuses and justify
their actions in the name of regal authority. After they depart,

the priests and the people mourn, but find solace in knowing that as long as human beings are willing to die for the faith, the Church will triumph.

Murder in the Cathedral is a modern morality play, steeped in the values and the passions of the Middle Ages and structured like a classical Greek tragedy with a chorus of lamenting women and a doomed hero meeting his fate with courage.

The Family Reunion (1939)

The main theme of *The Family Reunion* is the decay of an upper-class English family. The *Oresteia* of Aeschylus is the model for the play. The widowed, elderly, and ailing Amy, Lady Monchensey, wants only to save Wishwood, the ancestral family estate. As she and her siblings await the arrival of her three sons for her birthday party, they lament the fact that the younger generation has become decadent. The first son, Harry, arrives and is agitated and impatient with the old people. He is in the midst of soul-searching after pushing his wife overboard from a transatlantic liner. People believe that the wife committed suicide, but they are concerned with Harry's mental state too, for it is his duty to take over the estate from his feeble mother.

A policeman enters to inform the family that son John was injured in an auto accident and cannot attend the party. The third son, Arthur, has also had an accident and is under arrest for drunk driving.

Harry learns from an aunt that his father once planned to kill his mother when she was pregnant with Harry, but the aunt talked him out of it. Coming to understand himself better and the cause of the furies that seem to torment him, Harry decides to leave the estate, which angers his mother. But soon the mother and the aunt share the fact that they too have known the furies that haunt the family. Amy realizes that the family and the estate have been cursed, and as the birthday cake is brought out she dies. The play ends as the family turns to discussing her will.

The Cocktail Party (1949)

The Cocktail Party is a comedy in verse. Eliot comments on modern civilization through a play about a gathering of middle-class friends, most of whom are dissatisfied with their partners and looking for exchanges. Modern times are boring, people are selfish and vacuous, and nothing can be done about it except to laugh at the silly people and the trouble they make for themselves in romantic or sexual situations.

In a posh London flat Edward Chamberlayne and his wife Lavinia are giving a cocktail party, but Lavinia is not present. Edward makes up the excuse that she is visiting an ill aunt. In reality, she seems to have left her bumbling husband without explaining why. Eventually, and after much chit-chat, the guests leave, except for a stranger. He and Edward drink on for a while, and soon Edward is confiding in the stranger who points out that it might be a good thing that Lavinia left Edward since she was a difficult person to live with. But Edward wants her to return, and the stranger reassured him that Lavinia will return in twenty-four hours if Edward will not seek explanations.

Celia, a young woman who had been at the party, figures out that Lavinia has left Edward, and she believes this is the time for Edward to divorce his wife and marry her. But Edward is indecisive and fainthearted. The next day the stranger returns to the flat and informs Edward that by wanting his wife back he has made a mess of many lives, as all of the party guests were in the process of getting in and out of relationships with each other. Celia, for example, has lost an opportunity with Peter, who was in love with her, but now no longer loves Edward whom she sees as middle aged and ineffectual.

Lavinia, who has been stirring things up with a series of provocative telegrams, returns to the flat but is met by Edward's silence. The next scene is in the office of a noted physician, whom Edward is seeing because he thinks he is having a nervous breakdown. The physician turns out to be the stranger at the party. Edward confesses that he needed his wife back because he could not run his life without her strong hand. Lavinia is brought in and both parties admit infidelities. The score is even. The last scene is another cocktail party at the Chamberlaynes two years later. Pretty much the same old crowd is there, and the married couple is smugly wrapped in their old relationship. The audience is left to reflect on how superficial modern society is.

Additional Reading

Chiari, Joseph. *T. S. Eliot: Poet and Dramatist.* New York: Barnes and Noble, 1973.

Eliot, T. S. *Complete Plays.* New York: Harcourt, Brace, World, 1969.

Headings, Philip Ray. *T. S. Eliot.* New York: Twayne, 1964.

Jones, David Edward. *The Plays of T. S. Eliot.* Toronto: University of Toronto Press, 1960.

Sean O'Casey (1888–1953)

Sean O'Casey was one of the giants of modern Irish drama. His Dublin trilogy, *The Shadow of a Gunman* (1922), *Juno and the Paycock* (1924), and *The Plough and the Stars* (1926), changed Irish drama forever because they brought the voices of the tenement dwellers of Dublin on to the stage of the National Theatre of Ireland: the Abbey Theatre. The background to these great dramas were the three cataclysmic events of early–twentieth-century Irish history: the Easter Rising of 1916 (*The Plough and the Stars*), the War of Independence, 1919 to 1921 (*The Shadow of a Gunman*), and the Irish Civil War, 1921 to 1923 (*Juno and the Paycock*). O'Casey's dramatic mode was tragicomedy.

But these plays were written for Lady Gregory, William

Butler Yeats, and Dublin's Abbey Theatre, not for the London stage. When Lady Gregory and Yeats turned down O'Casey's next play, *The Silver Tassie* (1929), because the play had production requirements the Abbey could not meet and because Yeats did not like World War I plays, O'Casey took *The Silver Tassie* and himself to England where he lived in self-exile for the rest of his life. There, despite the fact that he wrote a dozen more plays, his career as a dramatist waned. In part because he changed his dramatic style from naturalism to expressionism, he never had the kind of impact on British drama that he had had on early modern Irish drama.

O'Casey was born in the teeming slums of Dublin. His education was minimal, partly because he was afflicted with poor eyesight. O'Casey worked as a laborer until he was almost forty and a successful playwright. His politics were always on the left, and he was much influenced by Jim Larkin, Ireland's most important labor leader. In 1927 O'Casey married Eileen Carey, an Irish actress making her career on the London stage.

O'Casey's plays written for the British theater include *Purple Dust* (1940, produced in 1945), a play influenced by Shaw in which a wealthy Englishman is determined to convert an Irish village to his values; *The Bishop's Bonfire* (1955) and *The Drums of Father Ned* (1958), plays influenced by Brechtian agitprop; and his last play, *The Scythe and the Sunset* (1958), a reworking of his epic Irish success *The Plough and the Stars*. O'Casey spent much of his last years writing his six-volume autobiography.

MAJOR PLAY ON THE
BRITISH STAGE

The Silver Tassie (1929)

The tassie is a silver cup awarded to a star football (soccer) player, Harry Heegan, who then goes off to serve in World War I. He is wounded in the trenches and returns a disabled and

embittered veteran. Act 1 shows Harry at the height of his career and in the prime of his life. The second act is set on a battlefield in France. It is a powerful piece of expressionist theater
and a moving visual poem of despair for the horror and suffering war imposes on human beings. Unfortunately, the act is
out of keeping stylistically with the rest of the drama. Acts 3
and 4 have Harry paralyzed and confined to a wheelchair. At a
dance in which he is unable to participate, he destroys the silver tassie, symbol of his youth and innocence, out of frustration and deep anger at how life has betrayed his youth and his
promise.

The Silver Tassie is an effective piece of antiwar propaganda,
written during the burgeoning peace movement of the late 1920s.

Additional Reading

Hunt, Hugh. *Sean O'Casey.* Dublin: Gill and Macmillan, 1980.

O'Casey, Sean. *Collected Plays.* 4 vols. London: Macmillan, 1949–51.

O'Connor, Gary. *Sean O'Casey: A Life.* New York: Atheneum, 1988.

Sternlicht, Sanford. *A Reader's Guide to Modern Irish Drama.* Syracuse, N.Y.:
    Syracuse University Press, 1998.

Enid Bagnold (1889–1981)

Enid Bagnold was best known as a novelist. Her most famous
novel is *National Velvet* (1935), the story of a racehorse, which de-
lights adolescents to this day. She was the daughter of a British
Army officer. She studied drawing and painting at the Walter
Sickert School. When World War I broke out, Bagnold volun-
teered as a nurse's aide at a military hospital in Woolwich, and
she saw service in France at the Battle of Verdun. In 1920 she married Sir G. Roderick Jones, the wealthy chairman of Reuter's News
Agency, and became a busy socialite. But quickly she took up
writing for several hours each day to escape her various duties.

After writing several novels, in 1928 Bagnold became interested in writing for the theater. She adapted several of her novels for the stage, including *National Velvet* in 1946. Later *National Velvet* became a famous film starring the young Elizabeth Taylor. Bagnold's most successful play was *The Chalk Garden* (1955). Other plays include *The Last Joke* (1960), *The Chinese Prime Minister* (1964), and *Call Me Lucky* (1967).

MAJOR PLAY

The Chalk Garden (1955)

The Chalk Garden is a Chekhovian play set in the English countryside, but, unlike Chekhov, Bagnold is affirmative and optimistic even though her play is about a girl stifled in an upper-class household and a garden where even flowers cannot grow because of poor soil. Mrs. St. Maugham, formerly a leader of a society that has passed from the scene, has retired to the countryside. She is frustrated by the garden that refuses to flourish. The rest of her attention is directed to her granddaughter, Laurel, sixteen, whom she would like to "grow" in her own image so that Laurel will preserve the memory of the once glittering Mrs. St. Maugham. Her own daughter was a disappointment to her.

Laurel, however, is a difficult young person. She is a pyromaniac who loves to light bonfires in Mrs. St. Maugham's garden. She also is a compulsive liar and given to fantasies that remove her from reality. When her mother remarried, she ran away from home. Fortunately a new governess, the mysterious Miss Madrigal, takes a liking to Laurel, who is, after all, the garden that needs cultivation, and Laurel will be replanted in better soil and flourish with her mother when she is no longer embedded in dead chalk.

The Chalk Garden is a highly symbolic play. It has religious connotations, implying that salvation is possible through loving care and communion with nature. Bagnold is committed to the life force. She is saying that life is worth saving and worth living.

Additional Reading

Bagnold, Enid. *Approaches to Drama*. London: Oxford University Press, 1961.

———. *Enid Bagnold's Autobiography*. London: Heinemann, 1969.

———. *Four Plays*. Boston: Little, Brown, 1971.

J. B. Priestley (1894–1984)

In his more than sixty-five years as a writer, J. B. Priestley wrote a myriad of novels, plays, biographies, essays, and journalistic pieces. He was a veritable writing machine (twenty-four novels and over thirty plays!) and the arbiter of middle-brow culture.

Priestley's philosophical belief that there is a dimension of time, different from commonly experienced time, in which all moments are recorded forever and are recoverable, led to his writing several expressionistic dramas about the nature of time. The first, *Dangerous Corner* (1932), is a country house mystery in which money is missing, one of three suspects is dead–a possible suicide–and the plot's consecutive events are linked to a mere chance remark.

The Linden Tree (1947) centers on a professor about to retire and the differing values of two generations revealed at a family reunion. In *Time and the Conways* (1937), acts 1 and 3 are set at a party at an affluent family home in 1919. Act 2 is a contemporary flash-forward to 1937, and the play poignantly contrasts the hopes and dreams of the partygoers, the reality of their future, and the actions that led to their respective fates.

Another significant time play is *I Have Been Here Before* (1937), where a mysterious German physician, suspected to be a spy, disturbs the other guests at a Yorkshire inn with his theories concerning time, which he insists reoccurs. Meanwhile a married couple having problems gets involved with a young man and that leads to murder. In the last of the time plays, the allegorical *Johnson over Jordan* (1939), the recently deceased Robert Johnson, a former businessman, steps out of his funeral and reflects on his career, the happy moments of his life, and what might have been. In the time plays Priestley attacked modern skepticism and loss of faith in a spiritual world.

Priestley's most popular farce is *When We Are Married* (1938). Three middle–class and very respectable Yorkshire couples, celebrating the anniversary day of their joint marriages, discover to their shock and horror that they were not legally married. Now each partner is faced with interesting new choices.

The morality play and psychological mystery *An Inspector Calls* (1946) takes place in the home of a wealthy family where a mysterious police officer interrupts to explore the possible connections between individual members of the family and a suicide he is investigating.

Priestley was born John Boynton Priestley in Bradford, Yorkshire. His father was a socialist schoolmaster who imbued his son with a lifelong concern for the weak and the poor. His mother died shortly after Priestley was born, and he was reared by a kindly stepmother. Priestley attended Bradford Grammar School until sixteen and then worked at various jobs while embarking on his writing career. At the onset of World War I, he joined the army infantry, was wounded three times in France, and left the army in 1919 as a lieutenant. With a veteran's grant from the government, Priestley went to Trinity Hall, Cambridge, receiving a bachelor of arts degree in 1922. After a year of graduate study, he became a successful, full–time writer.

Priestley married three times. His first marriage produced

two children and ended with the death of his wife by cancer. His second marriage produced three children and ended in divorce. Today, Priestley's novels, biographies, and essays are little regarded and seldom read, but several of his plays maintain a contemporary fascination and are often revived.

MAJOR   PLAYS

Time and the Conways (1937)

Time and the Conways is a play about the frailty of human happiness. It works better than any other of Priestley's time plays. The play seems to exist in the memory of Kay, a sensitive child of the Conways, as she contemplates the 1919 evening house party whose consequences affected all those attending. Her present time, and the audience's, is act 2, where in the same room, now somewhat seedy in 1937, the sad and disappointing results of the actions contemplated in act 1 are experienced. In a brilliant piece of theater, Priestley returns to the time and setting of act 1 for the final act, and we watch the characters make the fateful decisions contemplated earlier.

An Inspector Calls (1946)

An Inspector Calls is one of the most popular plays in the history of British theatre. It is set in 1912. The very rich Birling family is introduced as smug and selfish. When a policeman—Inspector Goul–calls investigating the suicide of a young woman named Eva Smith, the members of the family–mother, father, son, and daughter–are sure that the event has nothing to do with them, but in time we learn that they are all individually involved through selfishness, exploitation of the poor, blatant materialism, and contempt for human beings who are not of their class. The father, a manufacturer, dismissed the girl for going on strike. The daughter got the girl dismissed from her

shop–attendant job. The son got her pregnant. The mother refused her charity. All treated Eva Smith contemptuously. The
inspector is the voice of conscience as he relentlessly exposes
their complicity in Eva's death.

At the conclusion the play returns to the opening situation
as the inspector calls. *An Inspector Calls* attacks the pernicious
greed and callous indifference of early–twentieth–century capitalism. It demands compassion and kindness from the privileged and powerful toward the lowly and downtrodden.

Additional Reading

Cooper, Susan. *J. B. Priestley: Portrait of an Author.* London: Heinemann,
    1970.
De Vitis, A. A., and Albert E. Kalson. *J. B. Priestley.* Boston: Twayne, 1980.
Evans, Gareth Lloyd. *J. B. Priestley: The Dramatist.* London: Heinemann,
    1964.
Priestley, J. B. *The Plays of J. B. Priestley.* London: Heinemann, 1948–1950.

Noël Coward (1899–1973)

Noël Coward, brilliant dramatist, lyricist, composer, actor, and
director, was the ultimate twentieth–century theater personage.
Between the two world wars no other playwright was as uni-
formly successful as he was. Coward wrote more than sixty
comedies of manners, farce, historical drama, musicals, and re-
vues. Sophisticated, witty, suave, and outwardly very sure of
himself, he was also a gay man who suffered much of his life
because his image as a romantic leading man, his seemingly
heterosexual comedies, and the many love songs he composed
forced him to keep his sexual life a secret to the general public,
if not to his friends and colleagues in the theater. On stage
Coward's high camp was accepted by the audience as straight.

Noël Pierce Coward was born in Teddington, a London

suburb, to a poor family with connections to gentry. His father was a piano salesman. His mother, who took in lodgers to help financially, strongly encouraged her son to have a theatrical career. Coward's formal education was limited. His acting career began at the age of ten in a Christmas play performed at the Crystal Palace. Early fame came to Coward in 1917 with his play *Vortex*, about a well-born young drug addict who finds his mother's adultery impossible to bear and so he forces her to confront the reality of her behavior as he gives up his habit.

Coward's stage successes include the outrageous *Fallen Angels* (1925) in which two women make a date with a lover they shared before they embarked on their present dull marriages, and when he does not show, they settle for getting drunk; *Hay Fever* (1925), a madcap comedy about the eccentric, theatrical, and self-centered Bliss family; *Private Lives* (1930), a near perfect comedy about falling in love a second time with one's first spouse; *Design for Living* (1933), the story of a happy ménage à trois; *Blithe Spirit* (1941), in which the ghost of a deceased first wife must be exorcised so that the hero and his second wife can live happily ever after; and *Present Laughter* (1943), about an actor who struts like a peacock and maintains an unconventional household with the help of his former wife whose true worth he realizes in the end.

Coward the patriot wrote *Cavalcade* (1931), a large-cast panorama of British life from 1899 (the year of his birth and the beginning of the Boer War) to 1930 via the history of the Marryot family and their servants, the Bridges. Today, however, the play seems a chauvinistic spectacle designed for an emotional reaction.

After World War II, Coward was more popular with American audiences than he was with British audiences. But eventually for both, Coward's plays seemed slight and out of date. Audiences weaned on less sophisticated musicals and more naturalistic dramas did not catch the subtlety and satire in his plays and saw them as too superficial. But many of his comedies and musicals are still produced, his songs are still sung, and the film *Brief Encounters* (1944), for which he wrote the screenplay (he wrote several successful screenplays), remains a romantic classic of the British cinema.

Noël Coward received many awards and accolades culminating in his being knighted in 1970.

MAJOR   PLAYS

Hay Fever (1925)

The Blisses are an eccentric, artistic family living in a large country house. Each family member has invited a guest for the weekend without telling the others, so more guests arrive than there are rooms for them. The solitary maid is driven insane by the continuing demand on her services.

As elsewhere in Coward's drama canon, there is a lot of changing of partners. First of all, the middle-aged actress Judith Bliss, who is considering resuming her stage career, confiscates her daughter's prospective beau, a Foreign Office diplomat, who, having given Judith a kiss, finds himself embroiled in Judith's fantasy of an affair that must be revealed to her novelist husband. He in turn is pursuing the sexy young woman whom their son, a painter, has invited for the weekend. The novelist insists that the young woman, having flirted with him, must run away with him. Always looking for an excuse to be dramatic, Judith finds a role as a betrayed wife and a magnanimous woman willing to give up her diplomat "lover" to her daughter. In the end, to the astonishment of the confused guests, the family begins role playing from Judith's last stage success, a melodrama called "Love's Whirlwind," which of course is what *Hay Fever* is all about.

Private Lives (1930)

With its brilliant dialogue and titillating plot, *Private Lives,* a comedy of manners, seems to have captured the frivolity and thrill-seeking of the marriage-go-round of upper-class British society in the flapper age. The play is frequently revived and often serves as a star turn for a celebrity acting couple playing the parts of Amanda and Elyot.

Elyot Chase and his young bride Sibyl, on their honeymoon, have checked into a hotel room on the French Riviera. Elyot had been married to the now Mrs. Amanda Prynne. Unknown to Elyot and Sibyl, Amanda and her new husband Victor have moved into the room next door.

Amanda and Elyot spy each other from their adjoining balconies, and each immediately wants to move out of the hotel before their mates learn of the next-door neighbors. But the mates do not wish to go. Meanwhile Elyot and Amanda come to realize that they still love each other even after five years of separation, while their new mates seem less attractive after just a few days of married life. So Amanda and Elyot run off to Paris together.

But in Paris they quickly fall back to a love-hate relationship. Elyot is annoyed that Amanda had several affairs before remarrying, but he cannot understand why Amanda is bothered by the fact that he had affairs too. After agreeing to divorce and remarriage, they fall into jealous tantrums and a spectacular fight. Each retreats to a separate bedroom not noticing that Sibyl and Victor have entered the room.

The next morning Victor and Sibyl blame each other's spouses for the trouble. When all four are in the room together, Victor wants to fight with Elyot, who refuses to participate in such a cliché act. While Sibyl and Victor begin to quarrel and Sibyl slaps Victor, Amanda and Elyot slip away to renew their life together as ever-battling lovers.

Additional Reading

Coward, Noël. *Plays*. London: Eyre Methuen, 1979.

Gray, Frances. *Noël Coward*. New York: St. Martin's, 1987.

Hoare, Philip. *Noël Coward*. London: Mandarin, 1996.

Levin, Milton. *Noël Coward*. Boston: Twayne, 1989.

Morley, Sheridan. *A Talent to Amuse: A Biography of Noël Coward*. Garden City, N.Y.: Doubleday, 1969.

Graham Greene (1904–1991)

Graham Greene was one of the great British novelists of the twentieth century. Such works as *The Power and the Glory* (1940), *The Heart of the Matter* (1948), *The End of the Affair* (1951), *The Quiet American* (1955), and *A Burnt-Out Case* (1961) are classics. Greene came to drama at the age of forty-nine because he was excited by the challenge of the theatrical form: unity, precise structure, and the constraint of telling a story in three or so hours of dialogue and a very few scenes. Not surprisingly, the main themes of Greene's dramas are the same as his novels. Greene had a lifelong need to investigate and try to understand the mysterious relationship between a supposedly merciful God and sinning humankind, and, as a natural corollary, the relationships individuals build with those they love, fear, envy, need, or hate.

Henry Graham Greene was born in Berkhamsted, Hertfordshire. His first formal schooling was at Berkhamsted School where his father was headmaster. He went on to Balliol College, Oxford. During World War II he served in the British Foreign Office, and in his early years he worked as a film reviewer and an editor.

In 1926 Greene took instruction and joined the Roman Catholic Church in order to marry a Catholic woman he had fallen in love with. But his conversion proved to be true and indelible. Vivien Dayrell-Browning and Greene were married in 1927. They had two children, but the marriage was not a happy one, and they spent most of their lives apart. In 1930 Greene left the staff of *The Times* of London to make creative writing his full-time occupation. Greene lived a peripatetic life in which he sought out and found adventure and danger, always trying to locate islands of goodness and hope even as they sank in a sea of evil.

Three of Greene's seven plays found degrees of success on the professional stage. *The Living Room* (1953) revolves around a suicide, an act of despair that always fascinated Greene. In the play a woman who cannot make happy those whom she loves and who depend on her takes her own life to make them understand what she sees as the reality of existence. In *The Potting Shed* (1957), an unhappy boy tries to hang himself but is restored to life by a priest's great sacrifice to God: his faith. This play is based on Greene's attempted suicide as an unhappy schoolboy. *The Complaisant Lover* (1959) is an unconventional domestic comedy with dark overtones in which a wife wishes to keep both her husband and her lover.

Greene's true calling was that of a novelist. The theater was an excursion for him. The very nature of his peripatetic life and philosophical searching precluded a continuing exploration of, and devotion to, drama.

MAJOR PLAY

The Complaisant Lover (1959)

The Complaisant Lover is Greene's most satisfying play. The comedy explores the not so unusual tension between sexual needs and the restrictions of conventional morality. The wife of a dentist, Mary Rhodes, has a lover, a passionate and possessive bookseller. Mary loves her husband, too, even though he is immature and clownish. The husband, despairing over the knowledge that his wife is having an affair and indeed needs it, plans to commit suicide, but he comes to the conclusion that if one truly loves another, one gives that loved one what is needed. It is the bookseller who is outraged by the solution–a ménage à trois–but in the end he is convinced of the wisdom and the generosity of the dentist's proposal. Greene's solution to the moral problem essayed in the play is unconventional and was disturbing to mid-twentieth-century audiences, although not so shocking today.

Additional Reading

Greene, Graham. *Collected Plays.* Hammondsport, U.K.: Penguin, 1985.
Sheldon, Michael. *Graham Greene: The Man Within.* London: Heinemman, 1994.
Walling, Gerald C. *Graham Greene: A Study of Four Plays.* Peter Lang, 1992.

Emlyn Williams (1905–1987)

George Emlyn Williams was not only a successful playwright but a distinguished actor. He was born near Mostyn, Flintshire, Wales. His first language was Welsh. His father had several jobs in his life including coal mining. It was expected that when Williams was twelve he would go down into the mines, but thanks to encouragement from Sarah Grace Cooke, a school-mistress and social worker who saw the potential in the boy, he prepared for and won a scholarship to Holywell County School in Dorsetshire and from there, through another scholarship, entered Christ Church College, Oxford. At Oxford he became active in the Oxford University Dramatic Society, and he de-cided on a career in the theater upon graduation in 1926. While at Oxford he had already begun dramatic writing.

Only four years later Williams had a hit play, *A Murder Has Been Arranged,* and his next success was one of his biggest, the perennially performed *Night Must Fall* (1935). It is a macabre melodrama in which a charming but psychopathic bellboy carries around the head of his murder victim in a hatbox and terrorizes a family until he is caught. Williams initiated the role on stage.

Williams was especially good at writing thrillers such as *Night Must Fall, A Murder Has Been Arranged* (1930), and the later *Someone Waiting* (1953). Williams's most memorable play is *The Corn Is Green* (1938), a semiautobiographic drama that tells the poignant story of how a Welsh boy is influenced by a devoted schoolmistress to read, study, and go to a university. In *The Corn Is Green* (1938), Williams essentially relived his adolescence by playing the rebellious but brilliant boy. A very different but likewise successful Williams play is *Wind of Heaven* (1945) in which Jesus Christ is reincarnated as a Welsh boy.

Eventually Williams withdrew from playwriting and concentrated on acting on stage and in films. His "well-made plays" had gone out of fashion. Williams married Molly O'Shann in 1935 and the couple had two sons. In 1962 Williams was made a Commander, Order of the British Empire.

MAJOR   PLAY

The Corn Is Green (1938)
Early in the 1900s the doughty spinster Miss Moffat has the idea of setting up a local school for the children of coal miners in an impoverished Welsh town, and she starts a neighborhood school for boys. She finds a diamond of a protégé in the coal dust. Morgan is very bright and full of promise, so Miss Moffat decides to educate him to win a scholarship to Oxford. She recruits the aid of a local squire and battles the prejudice of the locals against the "waste of time" that education is for a boy destined for a life in the mines. But Morgan rebels against the

discipline as he falls for a pretty girl, thus endangering his chance at success in life.

Miss Moffat senses that her relationship with the young man has been too intense and absorbing. But her genuine affection, courage, wisdom, and perseverance bring victory as Morgan achieves the scholarship to Oxford. This sentimental play still finds appreciative audiences in Britain and America. Two major film productions increased its fame.

Additional Reading

Harding, James. *Emlyn Williams: A Life*. London: Weidenfeld and Nicolson, 1993.

Stephens, John Russell. *Emlyn Williams: The Making of a Dramatist*. Bridgend, Wales: Seren, 2001.

Williams, Emlyn. *Collected Plays*. New York: Random House, 1961.

Christopher Fry (1907–)

For a short period in the mid-twentieth century, Christopher Fry's verse plays added a literary quality to popular British drama unheard since the Tudor–Stuart period. Fry, with his Quaker background, also tried and in part succeeded in adding a moral dimension to the drama as he wrestled with the all-pervading dilemma: which action taken is right, and which is wrong? The path for Fry's literary achievement had been opened by T. S. Eliot's *Murder in the Cathedral* (1935).

Christopher Fry Harris was born in Bristol to religious parents. His father, an architect, served as a lay missionary in the Bristol slums, and his mother, whose maiden name was Fry, infused her son with her Quaker pacifist values. His father died while Fry was young, and his mother took in boarders so that she could afford to send her son to Bedford Modern School. At eighteen he quit formal education to work as a kindergarten teacher. At this time he began to use Fry as his surname out of respect for his mother's beliefs and sacrifices for him.

Beginning in 1927 Fry worked in and out of regional theaters. In 1936 he married Phyllis Hart, a journalist. They had one son. Two years later a small legacy allowed Fry to concentrate on playwriting. When World War II broke out, Fry was a conscientious objector, but he served in the Pioneer Corps fighting fires in the Blitz and clearing wreckage after air raids. After the war he returned to regional theater, but in 1947 *A Phoenix Too Frequent* had a successful fringe performance. The next year *The Lady's Not for Burning* was a great hit, and Fry could now devote his life to writing and adapting plays. He also wrote several outstanding television plays and miniseries.

Fry's many honors include the Queen's Gold Medal for Poetry, awarded in 1962. In 1988 Fry received an honorary doctor of letters degree from Oxford University.

Fry's most important plays shimmer with brilliant poetry and are vivid with historical color. As in Shaw's work, they feature strong-willed characters who battle with each other. They are message plays affirming the values of peace, love, and compassion. Fry loves life, and he sees it as a great gift to be used generously. *A Phoenix Too Frequent* (1946) is a one-act play about a young Roman widow who plans to fast to the death for love of her late husband. She waits for death by his body in the cemetery. But soon the life force exerts itself as she and a romantic young soldier share his food and agree to substitute the husband's body for a corpse he was supposed to guard with his life and had failed to do so. Young love triumphs over the conventions of death.

The Lady's Not for Burning (1948) is a comedy in which the life force again wins out over the death wish and a young woman does not go to the stake. *Venus Observed* (1950) has a traditional father–son–young woman love triangle. The Duke of Altair asks his son Edgar to select a wife for him from among three candidates, but the son falls in love with his choice, the daughter of the father's bailiff. Father and son battle for the young woman, but of course youth must win out and middle age be disappointed.

The morality play *A Sleep of Prisoners* (1951) is set in a church and often performed in one. Exhausted modern soldiers who are prisoners of war fall asleep. In their dreams they act out positions on violence and war–playing characters from the Old Testament.

The Dark Is Light Enough (1954) is set in a Hungarian mansion in 1848, the famous year of European revolutions, as the Hungarians are involved in a futile revolt. A compassionate, mature Austrian countess, Rosmarin Ostenburg, comes into the presence of death in war, and is willing to give up her life for another in order to show how necessary it is to recognize that every human life must be respected for the grace that is within.

M A J O R   P L A Y

The Lady's Not for Burning (1948)

The brilliantly written verse comedy is set in the late Middle Ages, the fifteenth century. A deeply depressed soldier of fortune, Thomas Mendip, feels he has nothing to live for. Life is meaningless and sordid. He sees an opportunity to get the superstitious witch–hunting townsfolk to execute him by confessing to a murder of an old man, although he did not do it. He is even willing to identify himself as the devil. However, the authorities refuse to hang the soldier simply because he wants to die. Instead they torture him to make him stop confessing.

Meanwhile, Jennet Jourdemayne, a wealthy young orphan and a pragmatist who refuses to accept abstractions, is condemned to be burned at the stake because she denies being a witch who has turned the murdered man into a dog. The mayor wants an excuse to execute her so he can confiscate her property. She wants to live and she mistakenly comes to believe that the soldier's desire for death was to save her life. Thomas is condemned to go to a party to see what life is all about. He consents as long as he can go with Jennet. She grows fond of him, and he of her. The soldier and the woman both now have something worth living for.

Fortunately, the "dead" man was not dead, but merely sleeping off a drunk. The young lovers are allowed to slip away, and the new dawn, which was supposed to herald death, opens their rosy future and is their beacon of hope.

Additional Reading

Fry, Christopher. *Selected Plays*. New York: Oxford University Press, 1986.
Leeming, Glenda. *Christopher Fry*. Boston: Twayne, 1990.
Roy, Emil. *Christopher Fry*. Carbondale: University of Southern Illinois Press, 1968.

Rodney Ackland (1908–1991)

The work of this bisexual playwright has been sadly and wrongly neglected, but now his achievements have been recognized by the National Theatre. Rodney Ackland's early plays, mainly tragicomedies such as *Strange Orchestra* (1931), *Birthday* (1934), and *After October* (1936), contrast easygoing but shoddy Bohemia with the hypocrisy in the supposedly respectable middle-class home. In the 1930s he was referred to as the English Chekhov, although his subject–London society between the world wars–seemingly had little to compare with the late-nineteenth-century landed class in Russia. Yet, as lovers in Ackland's plays often hurt each other, and brilliantly drawn characters find themselves disillusioned and cast off, the comparison to Chekhow seems valid, especially because the plays often end with hope for what tomorrow brings. Of course, when Ackland tried to bring gay and lesbian themes into his plays, censorship and the producers forced him to cut them out.

The Dark River (1941), Ackland's best play, portrays Britain in the fearful early days of World War II. The great, wide world, truly an awful place in the mid-twentieth century, finally entered the realm of Ackland's drama. The fascists are at the gate and the fight for survival has begun.

Ackland was born Norman Ackland Bernstein in Essex. His mother was an actress and his father a failed businessman. He studied at the Central School of Speech Training and Dramatic Art in London. Ackland worked at many jobs before he was able to make a living in the theater and films. He had male lovers, but at a party he met Mabbe Lonsdale, the daughter of the playwright Frederick Lonsdale. They fell in love, married in 1952, and lived a hectic life together for twenty years. When Mabbe died in 1972, Ackland returned to a gay lifestyle. He died broke, forgotten, and angry at his neglect by the theatrical world.

Rodney Ackland was also an actor and a stage director, a writer of screenplays and television scripts, and even a director of films.

Additional Reading
Ackland, Rodney. *Plays*. London: Oberon, 1997.

Terence Rattigan (1911–1977)

Terence Rattigan was a very successful playwright whose reputation rose and fell and rose again with the changing tastes of the British theatergoing public. He was a craftsperson of the theater who built his plays carefully on the twin pillars of character and plot. Rattigan was particularly skilled in exposition, that is, getting expository information out to the audience as quickly, clearly, and efficiently as possible. Terence Rattigan was at his best when writing strong emotions into his characters. Scintillating dialogue was not his forte. He saw British life as often joyless, rigid, and repressive. Perhaps Rattigan's ultimate subject was the repression of middle-class Englishmen.

Terence Rattigan's life, like Noël Coward's, was a lie. He was a gay man who had to pretend that he was heterosexual in order to keep his audience. Also like Coward, he became more conservative as he became famous and wealthy. Although Coward's and Rattigan's personal relationships were protected in various ways, they did little or nothing to support the cause of justice and equality for gay and lesbian people. Critics now consider that some of Rattigan's heterosexual characters and their experiences were stand-ins for gay characters and relationships.

Terence Mervyn Rattigan was born in Kensington, London, and educated at Harrow and Trinity College, Oxford, from where the scholarship student departed in 1933 without a degree. His father was a career diplomat and a womanizer. His mother was a Dublin-born Irish woman whose father was a successful attorney.

Rattigan began writing plays at Harrow and continued playwriting in Oxford. These plays were his apprenticeship to a career he chose early on. He left Oxford without a degree because a play, *First Episode* (1933), that he had written with another student was produced in the West End, and he felt that he could make a living without the degree. The play was a flop, and Rattigan came back to his parents' home to spend two years writing. The resulting comedy *French without Tears* (1936) made the investment in time worthwhile.

During World War II, Rattigan first served in the Foreign Office and then in the Coastal Command of the Royal Air Force as a flight lieutenant from 1940 to 1945. Despite his upper-middle-class background, Ratigan's initial politics were left wing, and after the war he became a pacifist. Both of these positions probably arose out of opinions he shared with many, if not most, former service people about the need for a more egalitarian society and about the futility and waste of war.

Rattigan used his RAF experience in writing *Flare Path* in 1942, a play about the experience of women in war waiting for, and worrying about, their men. The romantic drama was a success, as were his next two plays: *While the Sun Shines* (1943), a very clever farce about three servicemen sharing a flat and variously involved with the same woman; and *Love in Idleness* (1944; American title: *O Mistress Mine*), about a left-wing, seventeen-year-old boy who finds his mother having an affair with a married man. By this time, Rattigan was a master of the well-made play. But Rattigan became a writer to reckon with because of *The Winslow Boy* (1946), the story of a father's struggle, just prior to World War I, to clear his son, a naval cadet, from a charge of petty theft that would have ruined his life.

Other hits include *The Browning Version* (1948), a play about an unpopular schoolmaster, his unfaithful wife, and a surprisingly sympathetic student; *The Deep Blue Sea* (1952), the story of a woman destroyed by her uncontrollable love for a decadent philanderer; and the poignant *Separate Tables* (1954), a pair of one-act plays set in a small seaside hotel where in the stronger second piece two lonely people, a phony ex-army major and a sexually repressed spinster, share humiliations: he for being caught touching a woman in a cinema (in the original, censored version accosting men in a public toilet), and she beleaguered by her controlling mother. Also successful were *Ross* (1960), which tells part of the story of the life of Lawrence of Arabia, and *A Bequest to the Nation* (1970), a powerful drama that depicts Admiral Nelson's great passion for his lover, Lady Hamilton.

Rattigan was also a successful screen and television writer. In 1958 Rattigan became a Commander, Order of the British Empire, and in 1971 he was knighted.

MAJOR PLAYS

The Winslow Boy (1946)

The Winslow Boy is a play that John Galsworthy would have especially admired. It is riveting theater, it tells a story quite well, its subject is justice, and it has a moral: the righteous shall be vindicated. The play, set in Edwardian England, is based on an actual case that happened in 1908, a cause célèbre like the Dreyfus case in France. It shows the establishment as always hypocritical and despotic. Individual freedom is always in danger when governments place expediency over human rights.

Cadet Ronnie Winslow has been expelled from the Royal Naval College after having been accused of stealing a five-shilling postal order from a schoolmate. His father, Arthur Winslow, refuses to believe that his son could have stolen and, dissatisfied with the way the school investigation was conducted, demands a new inquiry, which is refused. He settles down to fight for his son's honor, regardless of the cost. After an independent inquiry, the matter is taken up by the House of Commons. But meanwhile Arthur has been ruined financially and his health has been shattered. Yet his stubbornness and moral principles win out. A civil trial is allowed. The brilliant defense counsel, a seemingly cynical barrister, proves to be dedicated to justice and fair play. Ronnie is acquitted.

The Browning Version (1948)

Set in the sitting room of Andrew and Muriel Crocker-Harris, *The Browning Version* is a classically constructed, long one-act play employing the unities of time, place, and action. No

Mr. Chips, Andrew is an emotionally repressed classics master who has placed his job over everything else, and who has been forced to retire because of his poor performance. It is his last day at the school. We learn that his wife is having a passionate affair with Frank Hunter, a science master, and that the Crocker–Harris marriage is arid and tired. The illicit couple cannot agree on the nature of love. For Frank it is caring and commitment; for Muriel it is sexual passion and prowess.

Muriel, who has had previous affairs, despises her ineffectual husband and humiliates him at every opportunity. Andrew was not good at establishing rapport with his students. He would have liked to be a popular teacher, but he mistakenly pandered to his students by playing up odd mannerisms so they could laugh at him.

But an unexpected event lifts Andrew's spirits. Taplow, a student, presents Crocker–Harris with a gift of a copy of Robert Browning's translation of Aeschylus's play *Agamemnon*, the classical Greek play about infidelity. Crocker–Harris knows the version of course, and he had once translated the play himself. Cruelly, Muriel states that the gift was a cynical attempt by the student to get a good report so he could leave the classics and get into the science class. Nevertheless, Andrew accepts it as a small victory in a day of total defeat, and the audience experiences pity for the broken teacher.

The Deep Blue Sea (1952)

The Deep Blue Sea is a play about a woman's need for a fulfilling emotional and sexual life. She is unable to find both with one man. Thus she is between the devil and the deep blue sea, the saying that gives the play its title. The play's protagonist, Hester Collyer, a woman in her thirties, is unconscious as the play opens. She has tried to kill herself with gas from the gas fireplace, but the meter ran out before enough gas had been expelled. Hester is married to a judge but left him a few months ago for a young, good-looking former RAF pilot named Freddie. He is good in bed, but a rather boring and lazy person. He would just as soon spend an evening drinking in a pub with his chums as make love to Hester.

A large part of Hester's problem is that apparently middle-class Englishmen do not accord high value to the sex act. One male character in the play is very sure that the physical side of a relationship is unimportant. Hester's husband, a judge and a decent man, just cannot understand why Hester is attracted to Freddie. Neither she nor her husband can actually say the word "sex" or its four-letter equivalent. He thinks that sex is separate from emotion, a simple body function, while she believes that sex deserves to be, indeed must be, an emotional experience.

When the play comes to an end, Hester has found the way to go on with her life through the counsel of a disgraced physician living upstairs. He too has been unable to fit in to conventional society. She goes to the gas fireplace again and once more turns it on, but this time, in a move laden with symbolism, she lights the fire, for hope has returned to life.

Additional Reading

Rattigan, Terence. *Collected Plays.* London: H. Hamilton, 1953–1964.

Rusinko, Susan. *Terence Rattigan.* Boston: Twayne, 1983.

Young, B. A. *The Rattigan Version: Sir Terence Rattigan and the Theatre of Character.* London: H. Hamilton, 1986.

9

World War II and After

Joan Littlewood (1914–2002)

Joan Littlewood was not really a dramatist. She founded several theater groups from the 1930s to the mid-1970s, the most notable of which was the Theatre Royal at Stratford in East London. She was the mistress of improvisational theater, a mode of theater that began with Italian commedia dell'arte, which came into being in the mid-sixteenth century. Early in the twentieth century, Luigi Pirandello gave it modern currency. She also "invented" what seemed like a new kind of directing, but which was really quite old. It produced "collaborative drama" in which a company is formed to build a play to performance, and all members of the company–director, designer, actors, and writer–contribute to the language and situations that may never reach a final form but that could be different with each production or even each performance.

Thus Littlewood influenced several modern masterpieces including the Irish playwright Brendan Behan's *The Quare Fellow* (1956) and *The Hostage* (1959), and Shelagh Delaney's *A Taste of Honey* (1958). Littlewood is best known for *Oh, What a Lovely War!* (1963), a Theatre Workshop farcical antiwar musical play that she created with the collaboration of Charles Chilton and help from several others.

Joan Maud Littlewood was born in Stockwell, south London. Her mother was unwed, and she was raised by a bawdy, storytelling grandmother. An avid reader from early childhood, she was a scholarship student in a convent school. Later Littlewood received a scholarship to the Royal Academy of Dramatic Art, and she worked as an office cleaner to add to the grant. In Manchester, working for the BBC's northern office as a producer, she made contact with the counterculture she sought. Soon she was connected with leftist theater groups, and she met Jimmie Miller, who later became known as the folk singer Ewan MacColl. They married and founded the Theatre of Action in 1934 and the Theatre Union in 1936.

During World War II, Littlewood and MacColl were blacklisted by the BBC as subversives. But shortly after the war, Littlewood was hired as a consultant by the BBC. McColl left her, and she began a thirty-year relationship with Gerry Raffles. In February 1953 they rented the old Theatre Royal, Angel Lane, East London, and that is where Littlewood made her great contribution to theater. Michael Caine and Richard Harris were among her young acting protégés.

In the 1970s Littlewood began living in France. She did much to change British theater. She loosened up acting, discovered new writers, found new faces for old classics, and brought fresh energy to the British musical. Littlewood's directing was much influenced by Vsevolod Meyerhold, Stanislavski's disciple; Adolph Appia, the Swiss designer; and, of course, the agit-prop theater of Bertolt Brecht.

MAJOR   PLAY

Oh, What a Lovely War! (1963)

Oh, What a Lovely War! depicts the horror and the carnage experienced by the British Army in World War I where among the ten million military deaths, 750,000 were British or empire men. With irony and parody, the play portrays the entire war including the actions of diplomats and generals through the old music-hall songs, dances, and conventions of the early twentieth century. Authentic songs of the period help create the euphoria at the beginning and the pathos that grew as the casualties mounted. Using Brechtian agitprop techniques, Littlewood had dance hall girls move into the audience throwing white feathers at the "cowards" in the audience, and young men ordered out of their seats (called up, so to speak) to man the trenches. Seeing and hearing *Oh, What a Lovely War!* is an unforgettable experience in nostalgia for a more credulous time, pity for all that youth wasted, and contempt for the ridiculous leaders and generals of many nations who sent the millions to their doom.

Coincidentally perhaps, the Great War began, and the play begins, in 1914, the year Joan Littlewood was born.

Additional Reading
Littlewood, Joan. *Joan's Book: Joan Littlewood's Peculiar History as She Tells It.* London: Methuen, 1994.

John Whiting (1917–1963)

John Whiting was a unique playwright for his time. Breaking with the omnipresent drawing-room comedy of the West End, his work was neither a part of the mainstream of British drama before the watershed that was John Osborne's *Look Back in Anger* (1956), nor was it in step with the radical and avant-garde plays of the late 1950s and the 1960s. His plays are reflective, philosophical, and short on action. His dialogue is extremely naturalistic to the point of appearing improvised.

John Robert Whiting was born in Salisbury, Wiltshire, and educated at the Taunton School in Somerset, as well as the Royal Academy of Dramatic Arts in London from 1935 to 1937. He acted on the London stage until World War II when he served in the Royal Artillery in the rank of lieutenant from 1939 to 1944. He also was a drama critic for *London Magazine* until two years before his death. He died before he could fulfill his promise as a playwright.

Whiting's best-known plays include *Saint's Day* (1951), an apocalyptic tale written in 1948. *Marching Song* (first performed in 1952, but written earlier) is a philosophical drama with much generalization about life, war, the military, and the nature of existence.

A Penny for a Song (1951) is a whimsical farce much influenced by Chistopher Fry. Like several of Shaw's plays, it celebrates traditional English eccentricity. Set in the period before the battle of Trafalgar when Napoleon was planning to invade Britain, a slightly daft baronet has a desperate plan to repel the French invaders. He dresses like Napoleon and, with a French phrase book in hand, he plans to order the French troops to return home. Unfortunately, he is taken for the emperor by his own villagers, and when his hot air balloon lands on a well in which gunpowder is stored, the villagers set the powder off and the baronet rockets over the countryside.

Whiting's last play was his most successful. *The Devils* (1961), commissioned by the Royal Shakespeare Company, is an adaptation of Aldous Huxley's *The Devils of Loudan*, a 1952 study of sexual obsession. It is a play about religious fervor and a case of hysterical demonic possession in a French nunnery. Its broad historical sweep and high theatricality are derived from Brecht's epic drama.

M A J O R   P L A Y

Saint's Day (1951)
Saint's Day, produced in 1951, was written in 1948. It is a confusing country house drama, more surrealistic than realis-

tic. In it an elderly poet plots revenge on the society that drove him out twenty-five years earlier. The villagers and the poet exchange hateful acts. The poet has a gun to protect himself that accidentally goes off in his hand, and the bullet kills his pregnant granddaughter. The village parson loses his faith and sets fire to his theological library. The fire rages out of control and the village burns down too. Then the poet is hanged by a band of marauding soldiers. The world of *Saint's Day* is apocalyptic. It is a portrait of hell in the British countryside.

Additional Reading

Salomon, Eric. *The Dark Journey: John Whiting as a Dramatist.* London: Barne and Jenkins, 1979.

Trussler, Simon. *The Plays of John Whiting: An Assessment.* London: W. Gollancz, 1970.

Whiting, John. *Collected Plays of John Whiting.* New York: Theatre Arts, 1969.

N. F. Simpson (1919–)

N. F. Simpson's surreal, Theater of the Absurd comedies resound with verbal humor and a sense that anything can happen to any human being any day of his or her life. His plays would remind French audiences of Eugene Ionesco and American audiences of the early Edward Albee.

London-born Norman Frederick Simpson was educated at the Emanuel School, London, and Birkbeck College, University of London, where he received the bachelor of arts degree in 1954. After secondary schooling and before going to university Simpson worked in banking, and during World War II he served in the Royal Artillery from 1941 to 1943, when he transferred to the Intelligence Corps. He was mustered out in 1946. Subsequently, Simpson worked as an adjunct college teacher and, for a few years, as literary manager of the Royal Court Theatre.

Four of Simpson's plays caught the spirit of absurdity and the public's eye. *A Resounding Tinkle* (1957) satirizes suburbia. An elephant has been delivered to the Paradock family's back garden, but it is too large so they decide to exchange it for a neighbor's snake, which is too small. This episode is followed by a mock panel of critics who pronounce against the play.

The farce *One Way Pendulum* (1959) is another satire on the British suburban household. In it a young man's ambition is to teach several hundred tell-your-weight machines the Hallelujah Chorus: if they can talk, then they should be able to sing. If he can bring them to the North Pole, their siren singing could draw vast numbers of spectators who will tip the earth's axis and cause a destructive new ice age.

Was He Anyone? (1972) is a satire on bureaucracy. The involved government departments fail in their duty to rescue a bookie's runner, Albert Whitbrace, from the Mediterranean Sea where he has been afloat after having jumped off a liner two and a half years ago. The government flies out a piano to him to keep him company, and he becomes such a fine pianist that the Leningrad Symphony Orchestra accompanies him in a concert. Alas, Albert is hit on the head by a life jacket thrown by a "do-gooder" and he drowns. So much for government bureaucracy and charity.

Additional Reading
Simpson, N. J. *The Hole and Other Plays and Sketches.* London: Faber and Faber, 1964.

Robert Bolt (1924–1995)

Robert Bolt's contribution to British theater as a playwright was small but important. Although a part of the conservative West

End scene, Bolt's socialist leanings and concern for the common person were genuine as evidenced in the commentator–Common Man–in his landmark play, *A Man for All Seasons* (1960), about resisting the power of the establishment. Bolt saw society as giving no fixed points of reference for right and wrong. Individuals are thrown back on their conscience. Brechtian devices also connected the play to radical theater.

Robert Oxton Bolt was born in Manchester to Nonconformist parents. His father was a shopkeeper and his mother a primary school teacher. He went to the Manchester Grammar School but left in 1940, feeling unready for the world. Thanks to a caring teacher, he obtained admission to the University of Manchester, but Bolt's university education was interrupted by wartime service with the RAF from 1943 to 1944 and with the Royal West African Frontier Force from 1944 to 1946. He received a bachelor of arts degree in 1949 from the University of Manchester and the next year he earned a teaching certificate from the University of Exeter. Bolt worked as a schoolmaster for several years and only started his writing career in the 1950s.

Bolt's first marriage, to Celia Ann Roberts in 1949, was dissolved in 1967. He married the actress Sarah Miles in 1967 and they divorced in 1976. In 1980 Bolt married Ann, Lady Queensberry, but they were divorced in 1985. Bolt then remarried Sarah Miles. He had been paralyzed by a stroke in 1979. He had four children.

Flowering Cherry (1957) was Bolt's first successful play. It depicts an office-bound man torn between his dream of radical action and his inability to make it happen. *Tiger and the Horse* (1960) is a play about whether a wife should jeopardize her husband's career by signing a petition against nuclear armament. *Gentle Jack* (1963) is an unsuccessful drama about clashing value systems. *Vivat! Vivat Regina!* (1970), a historical drama, depicts the relationship between Elizabeth I and Mary, Queen of Scots. Robert Bolt was also a very successful screenwriter.

MAJOR PLAY

A Man for All Seasons (1960)

King Henry VIII of England desperately desires an annulment of his marriage to Catherine of Spain with whom he has had a daughter. He desires to marry Anne Boleyn, who may be able to bear him a son. But only the pope can grant the annulment and he refuses. Sir Thomas More, a friend and trusted advisor to the king, is sympathetic to Henry, and is willing to step aside and not be a hindrance to the king's proceedings. But he will not swear a necessary oath that the king was in the right in seeking the end of his marriage. Because More is a most respected minister, recognized by nearly all the people as a just and righteous person, the king can be content with nothing less than the oath.

More struggles with pressures from the establishment. He wants very much to live. But he also wants to keep his integrity, and giving a false oath against the authority of the pope would destroy it. For a while More walks the razor's edge until his own clerk, Richard Rich, gives false testimony, and by that perjury More is condemned to execution for treason. He goes bravely to his death with a clear conscience.

A character named Common Man narrates the play and, chameleon-like, takes many parts as well as stage-managing the various scenes. His ordinariness stands in contrast with More's nobility.

The oath is the crucial center of the play. Bolt indicates that in a collective society the individual is generally debased into a usable and easily discarded commodity unless he refuses to accept that role by not buckling under to the establishment. In that regard, *A Man for All Seasons* is a secular parallel to Eliot's *Murder in the Cathedral.*

Additional Reading
Bolt, Robert. *Three Plays.* London: Heinemann, 1967.
Hayman, Ronald. *Robert Bolt.* London: Heinemann Educational, 1969.

Pam Gems (1925–)

Pam Gems's plays are full of energy. She paints her characters with broad strokes, and they come to life in three dimensions. Sometimes there is a formula to her work. In what could be called biographical drama, she takes historical figures and vivifies them, partly by setting them in the most significant moments of their lives.

Gems was born Iris Pamela Price in Bransgore, Dorset, and brought up by a mother and grandmother both of whom had husbands who died early. Gems attended Brockenhurst County High School, but dropped out at age fifteen. During World War II, she served in the Women's Royal Naval Service from 1944 to 1946. After being demobilized, Gems attended the University of Manchester, receiving the bachelor of arts degree in psychology in 1949. The same year she married Keith Gems, an architect who became a manufacturer. Pam Gems then worked for the BBC as a research assistant. The couple has four children. One child was born with Down's syndrome. Another child, Jonathan, is also a playwright.

The family settled on the Isle of Wight, and it was not until 1970, when Gems and her family moved to London, that she was able to find time and inspiration to write plays. The 1970s were a heady time for women. The women's liberation movement was at full throttle, and the fringe theater was at its liveliest. Gems was different from most politically active women. Like Joan Littlewood before her, Gems's background was working class. Also, she was middle aged, while most of the radical feminist women she met were middle class and about a generation younger. To her surprise, Gems found that the fact that she knew what it was like for women "before" was an asset to her writing and to her sisterly colleagues and friends. Within five years of moving to London, Pam Gems was an admired and respected member of a new generation of women playwrights.

Gems has written more than twenty-five plays. Her first success was *Go West, Young Woman* (1974), a play about American pioneer women and their experiences moving across the Great Divide.

Other well-received productions include *Dusa, Fish, Stas, and Vi* (1976), an episodic drama about various problems in the lives of the women in the play; and *Queen Christina* (1977), a play about coming to terms with sexual identity. This play brought widespread recognition when the RSC produced it. *Piaf* (1978) is a biographical play about the great French songstress's sad and sordid life. *Camille* (1984) gave Gems an opportunity to discourse on the masculinist fantasy of romantic love. *The Blue Angel* (1991) and *Marlene* (1996) are metatheatrical, biographical dramas depicting how Marlene Dietrich played the man's game as a sex icon. *Stanley* (1996) shows how the tensions of a triangular relationship affected the painter Stanley Spencer. *Deborah's Daughter* (1994) is set in North Africa and is based on the myth of Demeter, her daughter Persephone, and Pluto, the god of the underworld who abducted Persephone.

Gems's latest play is *The Snow Palace* (1998). It tells the story of a young Polish writer in the 1920s who drives herself to an early death in service to her art.

MAJOR PLAYS

Dusa, Fish, Stas, and Vi (1976)

Gems wrote *Dusa, Fish, Stas, and Vi* for the Women's Company. The play is about four city women in their twenties who are living together. Each woman has her distinct problem. Despite the fact that she was given custody of her children, Dusa's husband has kidnapped them. Stas, who cannot make up her mind about what direction to take with her life, works as a psychotherapist in the daytime and as a prostitute at night. Her ambition at the moment is to become a marine biologist. Vi is an anorexic drug addict trying to manage both problems with antidepressants. Fish, an activist, is the caring figure among the group. She helps the others but needs help herself dealing with the man in her life.

Things begin to look up for the women. Vi is getting better. Dusa's children come back. But the group is hit hard by Fish's suicide. It is extremely difficult for women to get control of their lives in what is still so clearly a man's world, for their lives are full of uncertainties. Custody of children, anorexia, and prostitution: the prices of a truce with men?

Queen Christina (1977)

Queen Christina is a wide-ranging, epic bio-drama. It provides Gem with an opportunity to explore in depth gender roles and the traps they can lay for a woman. It is the story of a lesbian woman, sole heir to the seventeenth-century kingdom of Sweden, which is at war. She has been brought up as a man and she has come to despise women for their weaknesses. But upon accession to the throne, the cross-dressing monarch comes under tremendous societal pressure to marry and bring forth a male heir. This need overrides her ability to plan strategy and conduct warfare. Forced to abdicate by the demands on her body, she goes to the abdication in a wedding dress and then travels in Europe. There she finds man–hating feminists repulsive because of their life–denying attempt to control their bodies by means of abortion.

Having converted to Catholicism, Christina is offered the kingdom of Naples, for which she becomes the masculine warrior again. But when she must kill her lover for betraying her army, she rejects all the binaries of the male–dominated world: male/female, master/servant, strong/weak, winner/loser. Although beyond the childbearing age, she begins to realize that female "weaknesses," such as the maternal impulse and non-violent behavior, are the world's only hope for salvation. Christina has found her true female nature.

Additional Reading
Gems, Pam. *Three Plays*. Hammondsworth: Penguin, 1983.

James Saunders (1925–)

James Saunders has steered clear of the mainline trends of contemporary British drama: the Theatre of the Absurd, kitchen sink plays, and the theater of cruelty. A major characteristic of Saunders's work is diversity. Like Shaw, Saunders uses the stage as a platform to discuss ideas. His best–known one–act play, the nonlinear *Next Time I'll Sing for You* (1962), apparently about the hermit Alexander James Mason, speculates on what the play might become if it ever got started. *Games* (1971) takes on political issues such as the My Lai massacre in the Vietnam War. *Bodies* (1977) is about two couples exchanging partners and exploring lifestyles.

Saunders is a compassionate person attuned to the moral complexities of our time. He investigates how couples relate to each other and manage to maintain commitment over long periods. He searches for the significance of loneliness and the meaning of death.

James Saunders was born in Islington, London, and educated at the Wembley County School and the University of South Hampton. He taught English in London schools until becoming a full-time writer. He married Audrey Cross in 1951. The couple has three children. Saunders has written extensively and successfully for radio and television.

Additional Reading
Saunders, James. *Four Plays*. Hammondsworth: Penguin, 1971.

Peter Shaffer (1926–)

Peter Shaffer has several valuable theatrical skills. He is a master of the well-made play, psychological drama, the epic, and stunning stage spectacle accompanied by music. His popular success has caused envy among other playwrights of his generation. But Shaffer's audiences generally have loved his work for their spectacle, melodramatic action, high rhetoric, and the wash of sound. They are never in doubt as to whether they are being entertained.

Shaffer's first stage success was *Five Finger Exercise* (1958), a drama of middle-class life in which Shaffer tells the story of marital strife in the Harrington family and how the rows hurt their nervous son. The Harringtons confide in Walter, a charming German tutor with a dark secret, who is brought in to teach their volatile fourteen-year-old daughter. Walter upsets the household as the family's weekend country house becomes a battleground. Like a Chekhov play, *Five Finger Exercise* ends without resolution but leaves the audience in a contemplative state.

Shaffer's next successful play, *The Royal Hunt of the Sun* (1964), is vastly different from *Five Finger Exercise*. Here Shaffer presents the tragic conquest of the Inca people of Peru, ruled by King Atahuallpa who believes he is a god. His antagonist is the Spaniard Francisco Pizarro. In the end Atahuallpa is killed and fails to come back to life, but not before the two antagonists have come to understand and even love each other, for both have failed in their own search for God.

In this play Shaffer begins to use a narrator, one technique of several to break through the invisible fourth wall of the stage. Shaffer studied Brecht and learned the holding power of narration as well the effectiveness of overt metatheater–keeping the audience fully aware that they are seeing a dramatization, and not relying on suspension of disbelief. What Shaffer decided to leave out was Brecht's agitprop support of his sociopolitical agenda.

In *Black Comedy* (1965), the characters behave as if they are in an unlit room (although the stage is indeed lighted). In it a young sculptor tries to sell a piece to an elderly and deaf art collector. He moves furniture back and forth from a friend's apartment in order to impress his fiancée's father. In true farcical fashion, the sculptor's schemes crash, but all is set right in the end.

Equus (1973) depicts a psychoanalyst's riveting relationship with a horse–obsessed patient, a part–time stable boy who drove a spike into the eyes of six horses. *Amadeus* (1979) discourses on the illusive nature of creativity by portraying the rivalry between Mozart and court composer Antonio Salieri, who sets out to destroy his young competitor because he has "heard the voice of God" coming out of an "obscene" child.

Lettice and Lovage (1987) is a comedy in which Lettice Douffet is a tour guide in a stately home where she makes up stories about its history. Her fibs are discovered by Lotte Shoen, a National Trust official, and Lettice is dismissed. But the two become friends and share some wild experiences.

The less successful *Yonadah* (1988) is based on the Old Testament's Book of Samuel in the time of David, and is replete with ambition, intrigue, rape, incest, and murder, with the villain, Yonadah, suitably punished in the end.

The Gift of the Gorgon (1992) is about the conflict between the son of a famous, deceased playwright and his stepmother. The son, an academic, wants to write a biography of his father, but the stepmother fears what his research will disclose and tries to block the project.

Peter Levin Shaffer was born in Liverpool to Jack and Reka Fredman Shaffer, middle-class Orthodox Jews. When the family prospered and moved to London, he was educated at St. Paul's School after which he did national service as a conscript coal miner in Kent from 1944 to 1947. He then attended Trinity College, Cambridge, on a scholarship, receiving a bachelor of arts degree in history in 1950. Upon graduation he spent two years in the United States, most of the time working in the New York Public Library. Returning to Britain, Shaffer held various jobs until the success of *Five Finger Exercise* in 1958, upon which he became a full-time writer. The popular playwright was made a Commander, Order of the British Empire, in 1987. Peter Shaffer's twin brother Anthony is also a playwright, the author of *Sleuth* (1970), one of the most popular whodunnits of the 1970s.

MAJOR PLAYS

Equus (1973)

Shaffer found the plot of *Equus* in a newspaper article about a stable boy in the north of England who had blinded twenty-six horses.

Dr. Martin Dysart is a psychiatrist treating a seventeen-year-old patient, Alan Strang, a stable boy. Dysart is trying to learn why the young man blinded six horses. The violent act seems beyond comprehension. In the consultations Dysart slowly delves down into Alan's psyche, stripping away the various defenses the boy has thrown up. He finds out that Alan worships horses in an archetypal primitive way. Alan has structured his life on his own mythology. The direct explanation for Alan's brutal act was because he botched the seduction of a girl in the stable. The horses, those jealous gods, had seen what happened, and he could not bear the thought that they could expose him. Of course there is no "logic" in the act, but passion, not logic, drives the youth.

Dysart, a traditionally educated, typically entangled human being, comes to realize that if he "cured" Alan, the boy's life would be devoid of spirituality, and he sees that his own life is pitifully bland compared to Alan's passionate existence.

Dysart stands for civilization with its order and conventions. Alan represents primal passions, fierce and uncompromising. As with other Shaffer plays, the conclusion is ambiguous, but the audience has come to understand and relate to the psychiatrist's experience.

Amadeus (1979)

This time the conflict is between two composers, one a feckless genius, Mozart, and the other a conscientious mediocrity, Salieri, who unfortunately has the power, in the court of Emperor Joseph II of Austria, to keep Mozart impoverished. The legend of the rivalry goes back at least as far as the early nineteenth century when the Russian poet Pushkin used it in his drama *Mozart and Salieri*. According to the legend, the jealous Salieri poisoned Mozart; in fact this element of the tale was fabricated fifty years after Mozart died.

In Shaffer's play, Salieri, in old age and insane, narrates the story in order to salve his conscience and save his soul through this confession. He knows he has committed a mortal sin. In his envy he chose to play God and kill the genius who represented the human spirit as well as innocent and natural humankind. Amadeus means "loved by God," and Salieri could not bear the thought that it is Mozart–rude, arrogant, childish–that God has chosen to sing through. In Mozart's last feverish days, he believes that Salieri is God's messenger, the Angel of Death, as he struggles to compose the unfinished *Requiem*.

Additional Reading

Giankaris, C. J. *Peter Shaffer.* New York: St. Martin's, 1992.

Klein, Dennis A. *Peter Shaffer.* New York: Twayne, 1993.

Macmurraugh-Kavanagh, Madeline. *Peter Shaffer: Theatre and Drama.* Basinstoke: Macmillan, 1998.

Shaffer, Peter. *Collected Plays.* New York: Harmony, 1982.

10

The Angry Young Men (and Women) and the End of Empire

Peter Nichols (1927–)

Peter Nichols was oldest of the playwrights who made their reputation starting in the 1950s, and who found the post–World War II Britain they inherited an unattractive place: class-ridden, full of injustice, and bruised in the aftermath of an exhausting and debilitating war. The atomic age, the cold war, and the sharp decline in world status seemed paralyzing. Their country was not the shining socialist city on the hill. It was a land of no hope and little glory. There was plenty to satirize if not to smash.

Peter Nichols is a satirist with a heart. Although he does not seem to have much hope for the human race in general, he has compassion for all. He dislikes the political and sexual hypocrisy of the left-wing middle class and he deplores snobbery.

Peter Nichols was born in Bristol and educated at the Bristol Grammar School, finishing in 1944. His Royal Air Force service from 1945 to 1948 took him to Egypt, India, and Singapore. After release from the RAF, Nichols attended the Bristol Old Vic Theatre School for two years and then studied at the Trent Park Teachers' Training College in Hertfordshire from 1955 to 1957.

Nichols taught primary and secondary levels for two years and then worked as an actor for five years prior to success as a playwright. Besides stage plays, Nichols has written numerous television scripts.

Nichols married Thelma Reed in 1959. The couple had four children. The first child, a daughter, was born severely spastic. The family had been living in Devon, but they returned to Bristol to put that child in hospital care. She died at age ten, never having spoken. Two more daughters and a son survive.

Nichols's plays are of two types: private domestic dramas and satires on social themes using Brechtian epic techniques and the music-hall format created by Joan Littlewood in *Oh, What a Lovely War!* The first type is represented by plays such as *A Day in the Death of Joe Egg* (1967), *Chez Nous* (1974), and *Passion Play* (1981); and the second type by *The National Health; or, Nurse Norton's Affair* (1969) and *Privates on Parade: A Play with Songs in Two Acts* (1977).

A Day in the Death of Joe Egg (1967) is a drama about a marriage stressed with a severely handicapped child. *The National Health* (1969) is a satire in which the real world and a fantasy world interact. Two groups in a hospital, the patients and the caregivers, act out their fantasies in a television soap opera entitled *Nurse Norton's Affair,* a melodrama about a black nurse in love with a Scottish physician.

Forget-Me-Not Lane (1971) is a three-generation play in which characters play earlier versions of themselves entering and leaving the present. The central conflict is the archetypal struggle between father and son. The comedy is the kind that accompanies pain. The protagonist, Frank, realizes that he has turned into the father he once rebelled against.

Chez Nous (1974) satirizes the sexual revolution in Britain. An affluent couple, Liz and Dick, have moved with their two children into a converted farmhouse in France on the money Dick earned from a best-selling book on sexual freedom. When two old friends, Phil and Diane, pay a visit, Dick and Liz learn that Phil had gotten their own daughter pregnant and that Diane was bringing up the child as her own. Sexual freedom is one thing in a book, but an altogether different matter when one's fourteen-year-old daughter is involved.

In *The Freeway* (1974), building a great north-south motorway results in a monumental weekend traffic jam that requires a number of marooned motorists to commingle and entertain each other, thus providing insights into the British character.

Privates on Parade (1977) is a play with music in which a team of traveling military entertainers illustrate the decline of Great Britain's post-World War II power. Army life is ridiculed and the concert routines of the sorry troupe are hilarious.

Born in the Gardens (1980) is a family play about a widow, Maud, and her three sons. Two are successful in the world, but the third, Mo, has chosen to stay home with his mother. Mother and son prefer living in the past to life in the caustic present, and the worldly sons cannot pry their brother away from that sheltered life.

In *Passion Play* (1981), Nichols deals with the vicissitudes of marriage once more. A married middle-class man feels he needs a lover in order to go on with his life. When he takes on a young woman, she soon tires of him, but the affair brings a cascade of troubles: rows, betrayals, reconciliation, and an attempted suicide.

The subject of the less successful *Poppy* (1983) is the Opium Wars of the mid-nineteenth century during which Britain forced China to buy vast quantities of opium thus causing widespread addiction. Nichols uses the conventions of pantomime cleverly, but blasting British commercial imperialism was out of date in the 1980s. *Blue Murder,* two one-act plays, opened in 1995.

M A J O R   P L A Y

A Day in the Death of Joe Egg (1967)

A Day in the Death of Joe Egg is a difficult play for an audience to sit through, although it raises worthwhile questions: mature people do ask themselves what they would do if they and their partners had a hopelessly handicapped, noncommunicating child to take care of for the rest of their lives.

In the play, Bri, a schoolteacher, and his wife Sheila have a spastic daughter whom they call Joe Egg. They fantasize that the severely brain-damaged little girl is leading a normal life, and they act out the roles of the physicians and caretakers involved in the family's life. The play shows the day-to-day problems and stresses the situation provokes. Bri clowns, makes jokes, and tries to lighten the grim atmosphere. Sheila believes without cause that she may have caused Joe's condition because she was promiscuous before marriage, and now she cannot or will not make love with her husband. Bri is beginning to fail in his teaching.

The outside world is hardly sympathetic. A male friend's well-meaning interference does not help. His wife cannot stand being in the same room with the handicapped child. In the end, Bri contemplates bringing about Joe's death by exposing her to the cold, but all he can finally do is run away from living death.

Additional Reading
Nichols, Peter. *Plays*. London: Methuen, 1995.

Ann Jellicoe (1927–)

Patricia Ann Jellicoe was born in Middlesborough, Yorkshire, and studied at the Central School of Speech and Drama in London where she hoped to become a director. After a period working in repertory theater, she joined the staff at Central School in 1952. She also founded and ran the Cockpit, a theater club. Her first produced play was *The Sport of My Mad Mother* (1958), an experimental drama about violent teddy-boy hoodlums and the brutality of British society. It was performed by the English Stage Company. The title came from the Indian mother goddess Kali, who symbolizes new life coming out of destruction. The drama was not a success. The British theater and the critics of the 1950s were just not very receptive to women writers, who really had something to be angry about.

Jellicoe developed a loose technique in her playwriting in an effort to make the dialogue seem improvised. Her long career as a director led her to value the expression of emotion over the appeal to the intellect of the audience.

Jellicoe's best-known drama is *The Knack* (1961). It marked her full maturation as a dramatist. *Shelley; or, The Idealist* (1965) is a quasi-documentary about the women in the great poet's life and how they fared in the male-dominated world of the nineteenth century. Jellicoe concentrates on Shelley's two marriages: to Harriet Westbrook and Mary Godwin. *The Rising Generation* (1967) was initially refused production because of its orgiastic feminism.

In recognition of her work as a director and in community theater, Jellicoe was made a Commander, Order of the British Empire, in 1984. Jellicoe married twice and has two children.

MAJOR PLAY

The Knack (1961)

Set in a recently painted room, *The Knack* is a comedy about four rational, intelligent, verbal people whose rationality begins to break down under the pressure of sex on emotions, fears, and insecurities. Tolin, Tom, and Colin live in the same house. Tolin is highly and successfully sexed, Tom is complacently satisfied with his sex life, and Colin, the landlord, is anxious about his lackluster sex life. A seventeen-year-old named Nancy comes on the scene, and Tolin wants her for his next conquest while Colin just wants her. He takes notes as he watches Tolin seduce Nancy.

Tolin wants Tom out of the house so he can bring in a friend, and he tries to manipulate Colin to do his bidding. But Nancy accuses Colin of having raped her while she was unconscious during an illness. A fight breaks out between Tolin and Colin when Tolin says Colin could not have raped Nancy, and Colin insists he did not but could have. Finally Tolin leaves and Tom looks after Nancy and Colin.

The Knack was a bold play for its time. It carries the audience away on its waves of energy and absurdist resistance to "meaning" in favor of feeling and individual interpretation.

Additional Reading

Jellicoe, Ann. *"The Knack" and "The Sport of My Mad Mother."* London: Faber and Faber, 1985.

John Osborne (1929–1994)

John Osborne's play *Look Back in Anger* (1956) changed the direction of British drama. British life was now under indictment. Osborne and many other playwrights, including Harold Pinter, Arnold Wesker, John Arden, and Tom Stoppard, brought the young back into the theater with their radical departure from comfortable, complacent, but competent middle-class drawing room drama that had dominated the mainstream British stage in the 1930s and into the 1950s. The revolution that Osborne fired up was political, but it was also a revolution in style. Yes,

the new drama was raw and radical, but now the British theater was freed from the shackles of the well-made play, happy
endings, star turns, and conventional staging.

John Osborne was born in Fulham, London. His father was
a commercial artist who died while Osborne was a child. His
mother worked as a barmaid. He was ill with rheumatic fever
as a child. At age twelve he was sent to the Belmont College, a
minor private school in Devon, from which he was expelled for
bad behavior. For the next ten years he worked at various jobs
including acting in repertory theater. Osborne began to write
plays, but he had no success until *Look Back in Anger* in 1956.
From then on he made his living as a writer. Osborne was married five times and had one daughter.

In *The Entertainer* (1957), Osborne makes brilliant use of the
music-hall genre to record his disillusionment with post-
World War II Britain. *The World of Paul Slickey* (1959), a protest
play insulting the establishment and critics, failed as a satiric
musical. *Luther* (1961) was Osborne's third major commercial
success. He borrows from Brecht the idea of using a narrator to
set time and place for each scene of the play. He made use of
Martin Luther's own words to create a powerful character
sketch of an Oedipal, troubled, and often ill person whose great
intellect and integrity drove him to rebel against the authority
of a corrupt Church and change the history of the world.

Inadmissible Evidence (1964) is the story of Bill Maitland, a
lecherous, alcoholic, pill-popping, wretched lawyer who gets
by through profiting on the misery of others. He is the young
and angry protagonist of *Look Back in Anger*, Jimmy Porter, in
middle age, facing his spiritual bankruptcy.

A Patriot for Me (1965) is the true story of Alfred Redl, a Jewish officer in the Austro-Hungarian army at the turn of the
twentieth century who has risen from a working-class background and needs to hide his homosexuality. Society drives

Redl to suicide because he is totally an outsider: Jewish and gay. Because one of the play's subjects is homosexuality, for five years the play was censored by the Lord Chamberlain, and it had to be performed in a club venue. *A Patriot for Me* is episodic and cinematic in its construction.

A Bond Honoured (1966) is about a clinical experiment in evil compounded with violence and blasphemy. The protagonist has raped his mother and lives incestuously with his sister/daughter.

In the social satire *Time Present* (1968), Pamela and Constance are flatmates. Constance is a member of Parliament. Pamela is an actress who has just ended a long-term love affair. Murray, Constance's current lover, is the father of Pamela's unborn child. The play is unstructured and serves primarily as a platform for Osborne's liberal views on sexual relations; nevertheless, the character of Pamela is particularly finely drawn and effective.

Hotel in Amsterdam (1968) is a play with little action but good dialogue on subjects such as love, friendship, the fear of failure, and the definition of goodness. Three couples, escaping a megalomaniac film director who employs some of them, hide out in a hotel and mostly talk.

West of Suez (1971) is a dark drama about a small group of English people in a villa on a subtropical island. It is an unsavory and unhealthy locale. The characters are nostalgic for the old England, but ironically they were all born out of the country in the vast reaches of the old British Empire. They represent a dying culture, and the play ends with a native revolt and violence.

In *A Sense of Detachment* (1973), Osborne breaks with almost all conventions of the theater. Interrupting plants provoke a battle between actors and audience as Osborne shows his disdain for the "philistines" he is supposed to entertain. In *Watch It*

Come Down (1976), a commune of artists–a film director, biographer, painter, a novelist, and others–living in a converted railroad station manifest most sexual combinations: husbands, wives, and lovers lesbian and gay. They have opted out of society, but society destroys them violently in the end.

West of Suez and subsequent Osborne plays were not nearly as successful as his earlier work. From 1976 to 1992 Osborne did not have a new play on the British stage. Finally *Déjà Vu*, a sequel to *Look Back in Anger*, was produced in 1992. In it Jimmy Porter is now thirty-six years older, living comfortably in Shropshire and vituperating against left-wing causes that he would have supported when he was a young man. Porter has become a philistine.

MAJOR PLAYS

Look Back in Anger (1956)

Look Back in Anger is a play filled with black humor and despair. It is set in a shabby attic flat in a Midland town. The protagonist, Jimmy Porter, comes from the working class. He has graduated from a red brick university that has prepared him for an establishment life, but he is contemptuous of that establishment because of the class barriers kept in place by the bourgeoisie. Therefore, he makes money by selling candy in a market. Jimmy Porter is angry because he believes that society is petty, mean, and hypocritical. He is disgusted with it, and he chooses to live outside of it even though that decision may hurt his wife and friends.

Porter is a revolutionary without any real cause. Frustrated, all he can do is hold his middle-class wife Alison hostage as a target for his frustration. But of course Porter's existence depends on the existence of that society he castigates. He tries to expose Alison to the realities of their lives in order to move her

out of her state of complacency, but in that attempt the under-
lying hurt that motivates his actions surges uncontrollably.
Porter hopes Alison will fight back against his tirades. She is
unable to do that, but her friend Helena can, and when Alison
is encouraged by her friend to leave and does so, Helena and
Jimmy live together. Jimmy was unaware that his wife was
pregnant.

Alison returns to the flat and Helena gives way because Alison has been badly shaken by the loss of her baby. Jimmy and
Alison revert to a childish world of role- and game-playing
that allows them to be affectionate in a way they cannot be in
the real world. For many Britons, especially the young, dissatisfied with the so-called welfare state, Jimmy Porter was the
personification of their frustration and anger.

The Entertainer (1957)

Like Jimmy Porter in Look Back in Anger, the protagonist
Archie Rice in The Entertainer is also a tormented hero-villain.
Archie is a faded music-hall comic entertainer, employing old,
bad jokes and poorly sung songs to woo small, bored audiences. Seedy Archie is disintegrating. His gigs are in fourth-rate
venues. He is totally cynical, and he assuages his failure with alcohol and by chasing young women even though he is married.

Archie's son is on active military service in the Suez crisis.
The extended Rice family is anticipating the soldier's return
from Egypt with a party. They are devastated by the news of the
young man's death. Archie is desperate as he is drained financially and his career is withering. He tries to stage a comeback
for his weak and befuddled father, once a beloved music-hall
star, but the elder Rice mercifully dies in the attempt. Archie's
affluent brother offers to pay to send the remainder of the family to Canada, but Archie cannot leave the decaying world of
the music hall. It is his real home and where he can live out his

fantasy of controlling an audience, achieving stardom, and being adored by fans. But Archie is only a morally bankrupt, grinning grotesque, bouncing around in a circle of limelight.

Osborne began his theatrical experimentation in *The Entertainer*, interspersing realistic scenes with music-hall numbers in a Brechtian manner. Osborne used the decline of the music hall–and three generations of the Rice family–as symbols of the decline of Great Britain in the first half of the twentieth century.

Additional Reading

Gilleman, Luc M. *John Osborne: Vituperative Artist: A Reading of His Life and Work.* New York: Routledge, 2002.

Hinchcliffe, Arnold P. *John Osborne.* Boston: Twayne, 1984.

Osborne, John. *Plays: One.* London: Faber and Faber, 1996.

John Arden (1930–)

Like Osborne and other of his contemporaries, John Arden searched for new forms and techniques to manifest his radical perceptions. The result is wild-eyed, flamboyant, excessive theatricality and the disappearance of an individual point of view in favor of an historical overview. In other words, Arden, like the younger Edward Bond, is a major follower of Brecht. But Arden also simplifies characters as if he were writing medieval morality plays. Arden's plays are distinctively eccentric and verbose, but always interesting to watch.

John Arden was born in the town of Barnsley in industrial and mining Yorkshire. His father managed a glass factory and his mother taught school. Arden attended a public school in Sedbergh, Yorkshire, for which he was stigmatized as an enemy by working-class children. From 1949 to 1950 Arden did military service as a lance corporal in the army's Intelligence Corps. Then he studied architecture at King's College, Cambridge, from which he received the bachelor of arts degree in 1953. For the next two years he continued architectural studies at the Edinburgh College of Arts, where he also began writing plays.

In 1957, while working as an assistant architect in London, Arden's *The Waters of Babylon* was given a Sunday night performance at the Royal Court Theatre, and Arden's career as a professional dramatist was launched. With the production of *Live Like Pigs* (1958), Arden gave up architecture to devote his life to the theater and to radical causes. Also in 1958 Arden married the Irish dramatist, actress, and political activist Margareta D'Arcy. They collaborated on *The Happy Haven* (1960), the first of several such collaborations. From the 1960s on, Arden was an active supporter of antiwar and antinuclear organizations in Britain and elsewhere in the world.

Beginning in 1972, Arden and D'Arcy began writing and producing Marxist dramas for and with amateur groups. *The Island of the Mighty* (1972) is a successful example of their collaboration during this period. Between 1970 and 1972 Arden converted to a more radical Marxism.

In the 1980s and 1990s, Arden wrote several novels, having given up mainstream British theater. Arden, a stubborn and principled Yorkshireman, has resisted the financial lure of screenwriting, where his political agenda would find no breathing space.

Arden's first commercial play, *The Waters of Babylon* (1957), is an antiwar play in which the protagonist Sigismanfred Krankiewicz is a Polish immigrant who works as an architect's assistant in London and also runs a boarding house. He is a pimp and a former concentration camp guard who will do anything to survive. Nevertheless, the audience has some sympathy for his struggle. Brecht's character Mother Courage, a woman who profits from the Thirty Years War while her children are killed, seems to be the model for "Krank."

Live Like Pigs (1958) tells the story of the Sawney family, gypsy-like nomads in Britain who move into a public housing estate in northern England to the dismay of their working-class neighbors trying to be middle class. Class conflict, so often a theme in Arden's work, results in attempted rape, vandalism, prostitution, and fights as the Sawneys fight the pressure from unsympathetic housing authorities to conform to the social norms and "fit in."

In *Serjeant Musgrave's Dance* (1959), considered by audiences and critics Arden's masterpiece, four deserters from the British Army wish to impress the residents of a northern English town in the 1880s of the futility of war. Unbeknownst to them, their leader, Serjeant Musgrave, has conceived a demonic way to do it.

In *The Happy Haven* (1960), a group of residents of an old age home battle Dr. Copperthwaite, who wants to experiment on them with an elixir-of-youth serum. Arden and D'Arcy provide no clear-cut judgment on the doctor or his patients. Both parties are locked into their respective agendas, and as the play ends, Mrs. Phineus, a rejuvenated resident, holds Dr. Copperthwaite in her loving arms.

The Workhouse Donkey: A Vulgar Melodrama (1963) is a comedy about corruption in a northern English town. An alderman, Charlie Butterthwaite of the Labour Party, has had his way with the town, but he is finally confronted by the new chief constable he has appointed. The constable is a letter-of-the-law person supported by the Conservative Party, who successfully does battle with the alderman.

Armstrong's Last Good (1964) was a major hit. It is a romantic, exciting history play discussing James V of Scotland and his efforts to control the clans and make peace with the English. His effective instrument is the poet-politician Sir David Lindsay, who finally hangs the cross-border raider and betrayer of all sides, Johnny Armstrong.

Left-Handed Liberty: A Play about Magna Carta (1965) is an historical pageant with the theme that documents and laws are only as good as the people who write them and the people who live under them.

Two collaborations with D'Arcy marked the end of Arden's relationship with mainstream British theater: *The Hero Rises Up: A Romantic Melodrama* (1969), which shows the great naval hero Admiral Horatio Nelson as vain, vulgar, and cruel; and *The Island of the Mighty* (1962), the story of King Arthur's vain attempts to unite a Britain, like the Britain of the 1960s, beset with quarreling factions.

John Arden has always charged the artist with political responsibilities. One of those responsibilities is to show the public both sides of a conflict. For Arden, simple answers to complex questions do not exist.

MAJOR   PLAY

Serjeant Musgrave's Dance

Serjeant Musgrave's Dance is one of the most powerful doctrinaire dramas ever seen on the British stage. It is an antiwar play with a savage twist.

Four nineteenth-century British Army deserters come to a northern English town. They pretend to be a recruiting party, but, having served the queen in colonial wars, and having seen and done much killing, the soldiers want to convince the townspeople that war is futile. Musgrave, however, has a secret plan not revealed until act 3. He wants to make the point that war and killing are wrong by executing twenty-five townspeople, including those in authority who support the army. In disagreement the deserters fight with each other, and one is killed before the town meeting Musgrave calls. At the meeting, Musgrave switches from endorsing army life to describing the horrible things soldiers do. The mad soldier does a dance of death with a skeleton.

Musgrave's plan fails as dragoons arrive. They shoot one deserter and arrest Musgrave and his last comrade. In prison awaiting execution, one of the deserters realizes that we cannot stop the plague of war and bring peace by more killing. But the miners in the town who have been saved now do not know what to do with their lives. In keeping with Marxist ideology, it is history not Arden who condemns the protagonist. History sweeps mortals along in its unstoppable current.

Additional Reading

Arden, John. *Plays*. London: Methuen Drama, 2002.

Gray, Frances. *John Arden*. London: Macmillan, 1982.

Malik, Javed. *Toward a Theater of the Oppressed: The Dramaturgy of John Arden*. Ann Arbor: University of Michigan Press, 1995.

Page, Malcolm. *John Arden*. Boston: Twayne, 1984.

11

Beckett's Pervading Influence

Harold Pinter (1930–)

Harold Pinter and Tom Stoppard have made contemporary British drama a significant part of world drama. Their plays are widely translated and performed around the globe. Both playwrights are indebted to the groundbreaking contribution to world drama that the Irish playwright and Nobel Prize-winning Samuel Beckett made in combining existential philosophy–an ontological vision of life as solitary, random, and absurd–and an antinaturalistic concept of dramaturgy, the prime example of which is *Waiting for Godot* (1953). Pinter first saw *Waiting for Godot* in London in 1956. Pinter absorbed much of Beckett except that Pinter's plays are, on the surface at least, naturalistic. But Pinter and Stoppard both are influenced by Beckett in their trademark transmutation of banal language exchanges into sophisticated battles of wit surrounded by pregnant pauses.

Pinter's characters experience loneliness, fear, terror, solitude, emptiness, despair, and the inability to communicate. They are often tormented by forces beyond their control regardless of their innocence or guilt. Pinter mocks reason. He has no faith in passion or the endurance of love. Value judgments like good and evil are either obscure, left to the audience, or totally banished. Thus Pinter's plays have a purposeful ambiguity that allows for interpretation and even argument.

Conventionally, plot in drama provides certain actions that bring a play to life. It folds character and idea into dialogue and progressive movement. In Pinter's work, plot slowly reveals an emotional state. Dramatic situation often replaces traditional plot. That concept is exciting in its freshness, but also limiting in its lack of the rising and falling action that proceeds from unfolding revelations through the alternation of suspense and surprise.

Harold Pinter was born in impoverished East London. His father, Hyman, was a tailor, descended from Portuguese Jews named da Pinta. His mother was the former Frances Mann. Pinter, an only child, grew up experiencing anti-Semitism and violence before and during World War II. When London was blitzed, Pinter was evacuated to the country with thousands of other children.

Pinter's education included local primary schools, then the Hackney Downs Grammar School from 1943 to 1947, and the Royal Academy of Dramatic Art in 1948. When called for military service, Pinter declined as a conscientious objector, not wanting to be a part of the cold war. He was fined for his decision.

In 1949 Pinter began his professional acting career, supplementing income with various nonacting jobs. In the early 1950s he toured with Anew McMaster's repertory company in Ireland and Donald Wolfit's classical repertory company in Britain. Pinter's career as a playwright began with the one-act play *The Room* (1956), set in a small, dilapidated flat from which the outside world seems menacing. *The Room* set the tone and coloration of much of Pinter's later work.

Pinter married the actress Vivien Merchant in 1956. They had a son, and were divorced in 1980 when Pinter married the distinguished biographer Lady Antonia Fraser. Pinter has worked as a director of the National Theatre. He has also made an important contribution to contemporary cinema by writing several outstanding screenplays; he has directed widely for the stage and acted in his own plays. His many honors include Commander, Order of the British Empire, awarded in 1966. Pinter has been a devoted activist for peace and human rights around the world.

The Dumb Waiter (1957), a one-act play, is a dark and menacing comedy about two hired gunmen waiting for the order to murder an unknown person. Pinter's first full-length drama is *The Birthday Party* (1958) in which visitors break down the protagonist by playing upon his fears while pretending to celebrate his birthday. They want to destroy his identity. *A Slight Ache* (1958) is a play about a man's psychological breakdown after blinding and squashing a wasp. His eyes begin to ache as the match seller appears, a man who may have raped Edward's wife many years ago and who now is seduced by her.

The *Caretaker* (1960) portrays two brothers struggling for power with a tramp trying to ingratiate his way into their house and lives. *The Caretaker* is the drama that made the critics recognize that Pinter was a force in contemporary theater.

The Homecoming (1965), one of Pinter's commercial successes, focuses on a savage contest over a sexually desirable woman fought by a family of men. In *Old Times* (1970), a play about memory, a husband and wife battle over a girlfriend of the wife who may also once have been the husband's lover. The trio talk over old times, but what they say may or may not have happened. The wife and the girlfriend may or may not have been lesbian lovers. Although the girlfriend seems to hold the power, in the end it is the wife who is in control simply because she is less interested in winning.

No Man's Land (1974) is about an impoverished poet who

tries to worm his way into the household of a celebrity colleague, but who is thwarted by the watchful servants who orchestrate their employer's life and minister to his homosexual desires. Ultimately, the servants control both poets' lives. *Betrayal* (1978) is about a love triangle that seems conventional until the audience realizes that the story is being played backward. It is one of Pinter's most popular and frequently performed dramas. *Family Voices* (1981), originally written for radio, is an epistolary play with a mother's and a son's voices instead of written letters, although the monologues are referred to as letters. The story concerns a young man who has left his rural home to live in a large city. He has located a room in a rooming house run by an elderly woman who weans him from his affection for his mother because she wants a foster son. The play is a Freudian parable about coming to sexual maturity. *A Kind of Alaska* (1982) is a about a patient with sleeping sickness who is stressfully disoriented because of a new drug that revives him.

As the 1980s progressed, Pinter's plays became more politicized, as in *One for the Road* (1984), in which the protagonist's home is invaded by soldiers who arrest him, murder his son, rape his wife, torture him physically and mentally, and then are kind to him in order to bring him to conformity. *Mountain Language* (1988) is a powerful one-act play in which soldiers of a dictatorship use bureaucratic doublespeak to victimize women waiting outside a prison for news of their missing husbands. *Party Time* (1991) is reminiscent of *Mountain Language*. In this play, women who ostensibly exist comfortably worry about people lost in the past: a husband, a brother, and friends who have disappeared into the clutches of a totalitarian regime. The "disappeared" have left a great void in their lives.

In *Ashes to Ashes* (1996), Devlin questions Rebecca, the woman he is living with, about her former lover, a factory owner. Rebecca relates the story willingly despite the fact that the relationship was sadomasochistic. As the play progresses, Devlin becomes more abusive, but when Rebecca also reveals that her baby was taken away as she was about to board a train, and that her former lover tore babies from screaming mothers, it becomes clear that Rebecca is a Holocaust survivor. Thus, obtaining sympathy, she gets the upper hand in her new relationship. In this cryptic way, Pinter finally confronts the Holocaust, an event and a theme he had written around before but never explicitly addressed.

Celebration (2000) is a comic satire on the coarse, greedy, and ill-mannered nouveaux-riches. Pinter sees as a source of moral decay capitalism's materialism and stress on the individual's right selfishly to acquire whatever he or she can. The parvenu insulates himself or herself from the suffering in the world and is only concerned with power and sex. In *Remembrance of Things Past* (2000), a police inspector, who is divorced and whose career is unraveling, finds a woman collapsed on the street on Christmas Eve and does not know what to do with her. These later plays, cryptic and enigmatic, have received less attention from the public.

Pinter's drama depicts the human condition as full of unexpressed fears, often from unknown or unexpected sources, that must be battled but are seldom beaten. Survival is the best one can hope for. The likely outcome is Hobbesian: domination, exploitation, and victimization.

MAJOR   PLAYS

The Dumb Waiter (1957)

In *The Dumb Waiter*, a short play, two workers are only killing time as they await someone in authority to tell them what their job is. The bumbling thugs try to cover themselves by responding to and attempting to fulfill impossible orders for exotic food sent down to them via a dumb waiter, a small elevator apparently controlled by the boss upstairs. Soon the audience realizes that the workers are thugs hired to murder a victim. Ironically, it turns out that the victim to be is one of them. Thus even the agents of evil are possible victims, or even inevitable victims. Comically the men rehearse their killing procedure.

The Birthday Party (1958)

The Birthday Party is about the subjugation of its protagonist, Stanley Webber, who is living sedately in a seaside guesthouse where he has been dominating his landlady. Two men, Goldberg and McCann, agents from an unknown person or organization, intrude on the birthday party Webber's landlady has thrown for him, and then proceed to intimidate and take control of Webber. The intruders personify some repressive or fascist government—a familiar experience to many Europeans in the twentieth century. Indeed, the situation is surrealistically Kafkaesque. After a night of consummate terror, Goldberg and McCann take Webber away in the morning. He is passive, submissive, brainwashed, and dressed in a respectable suit, ready for the new Orwellian society. Meanwhile, the landlady is unaware of her tenant's abduction.

Initially, Webber had struggled to hide his personal identity by being vague about his background and work. He has a right to his privacy and his individuality, but that is exactly what the state does not want him or us to maintain.

The Caretaker (1960)

In The Caretaker Aston and his younger brother Mick live in a house in London that both claim to own, but in fact Mick owns the house and Aston may actually live somewhere else. Aston rescues Davies, a frightened old street person, from a

fight, and offers him a little money and a place to sleep until he
can get himself back on his feet. Apparently, Aston has done
this before. Mick, in a bid for dominance, initially intimidates
and even terrorizes Davies, but before long he tries to ingratiate himself with the old man. Separately, both brothers offer
Davies a caretaking job in the house.

Aston, who usually speaks in clipped sentences, reveals in
what seems to be a studied speech that he has been in a mental institution where shock treatments caused brain damage.
Instead of sympathizing with Aston, Davies calls his benefactor
half crazy. It becomes apparent that Mick is his mentally damaged brother's caretaker, and Aston is the caretaker of his
brother's house. There was no need for a caretaker, but there
was need for Aston to find a friend and for Mick to have someone to browbeat and humiliate. Davies attempts to play one
brother off against the other, and in the end he does not get the
job, and Aston, roused from a stupor, tosses him back on the
street. The brothers, meanwhile, affirm their brotherly love.

There is comedy in *The Caretaker* as when Mick, Aston, and
Davies scuffle for Davies's bag, which turns out not really to be
his. Also, Davies reminds one of Beckett's tramps in *Waiting for
Godot*, and like that play *The Caretaker* is about relationships
under stress.

The Homecoming (1965)

Although a favorite of the author, *The Homecoming* is Pinter's
most controversial drama, partly because of its relative lack of
action and the intensity of its dialogue, but mainly because it
violates the audience's expectations for what is ostensibly a
family play in a domestic setting, an old London house. The action of *The Homecoming* takes place during twenty-four hours.

In the house of an East End London Jewish family live its
head, a retired butcher named Max, a hot-tempered patriarchal
type; his brother Sam, a chauffeur and a decent person; and

two sons, Lennie, a pimp, and Joey, a boxer. It is an all-male world. A third son, Teddy, an academic, has been in America for six years. Now he has returned to the house with his English wife, Ruth, who has not met her husband's family before.

Ruth claims to have been a photographer's nude model. Her sexual appeal is a threat to the power structure of the house, which is based on patriarchal conceptions of gender, and so Ruth is badly treated by Max and Lennie. Sam protests but dies. Soon the men in the house, especially Lennie and Joey, lay sexual claim to Ruth, and the play itself is sexually electrified in an ominous way. Teddy is going to depart for America again without his wife. The men plan and negotiate with Ruth to turn her into a prostitute working for them. Ruth cannot be a mother figure for these men, for that would give her unacceptable, matriarchal power; but forced into a "proper" servile position as a prostitute she could bring in money. Significantly, they have harnessed her sexual power.

But at the end Ruth uses her sexual power and the potential economic power she has to take control of the situation. With her husband out of the picture, she assumes authority and Max is no longer head of the house. Lennie the pimp, clever, streetwise, and verbal, has become the alpha male. The view of men and women in *The Homecoming* is frightening and distasteful. The play is a dark parable of the war of the sexes.

Betrayal (1978)

Betrayal is a play about the death of a marriage through infidelity. At a party in 1968 a man comes on to a friend's wife; she is interested, and they commence an affair, renting an apartment for their trysts. Five years later, the husband, Robert, learns about it but does nothing. Two years after that the affair ends. And in two more years the marriage also ends. What is surprising and innovative is the sequencing of scenes. Scenes 1 and 2 are in chronological order, apparently in the year 1977 when the marriage is ending and the lovers have parted. In scene 1 Jerry the lover and Emma the wife want to clarify their various betrayals. In scene 2 Robert and Jerry meet to discuss Emma's betrayals and bring the play to closure. Scene 3 occurs in 1975 when the affair ends. In scene 4, set in 1974, Robert, who now knows about the affair, betrays Jerry by goading and mocking him. Scenes 5, 6, and 7 take place chronologically in 1973 when the affair is in full bloom. Although Robert knows about the affair, Jerry does not know that Robert knows. Scene 8 is in 1971 when the affair is first blossoming. Scene 9 is set at the party in 1968 when the betrayal of marital fidelity and friendship occurs, and the tragicomedy of love and/or marriage begins.

The backward movement of the play with the spasmodic jerks forward results in a strong, even painful, emotional feeling of disillusionment in the audience, which is just what Pinter wants. The play also creates the sensation that one is seeing a film in which there are flashbacks as well as scenes moving forward chronologically. Ultimately, this brilliantly constructed and painfully comic play is an essay on betrayal, including self-betrayal.

Additional Reading

Billington, Michael. *The Life and Work of Harold Pinter.* London: Faber and Faber, 1996.

Cahn, Victor L. *Gender and Power in the Plays of Harold Pinter.* Basingstoke: Macmillan, 1994.

Dukor, Bernard F. *Harold Pinter.* London: Macmillan, 1988.

Gordon, Lois, ed. *Pinter at Seventy: A Casebook.* New York: Routledge, 2001.

Pinter, Harold. *Plays.* London: Faber and Faber, 1996.

Raby, Peter, ed. *The Cambridge Companion to Harold Pinter.* Cambridge: Cambridge University Press, 2001.

Peter Barnes (1931–2004)

Peter Barnes had an outstanding success with *The Ruling Class* in 1968. It seemed exactly the right play for that revolutionary year because it attempted to overthrow the power of naturalism on the British stage and hold the church–state establishment up to savage satire and deadly ridicule.

Barnes was born in London. His formal education ended after he left Stroud Grammar School to work for the London County Council and then to do military service in the Royal Air Force from 1949 through 1950. After the RAF he returned to the London County Council to work for several years until he was able to earn a living as a film critic and story editor. Barnes married Charlotte Beck in 1958. His career has including writing screen, radio, and television plays as well as directing in the theater.

Sclerosis (1965) satirizes the British Empire, an easy mark after the Suez crisis. *Bewitched* (1974) takes on a favorite Barnes target: England's class system. In the play the Spanish emperor Carlos II, a deformed, impotent, epileptic idiot, the result of generations of royal inbreeding, is flattered and obeyed by his courtiers. But Spain needs a legitimate heir, and so a young man is smuggled into the queen's bedroom dressed as a maid. But the assignation is exposed. In the end, the flattering nobles are crushed into happy caricatures of the crippled monarch. *Laughter* (1978) is about murderous villains like Ivan the Terrible who are compared with the Germans who devised and efficiently ran the death camps of the Holocaust. Barnes scathingly indicts humankind as he indicates that there was nothing unusual in the actions of the German torturers and murderers who created Auschwitz. Their behavior was simply that of people brought up in middle–class Western culture, where savagery and brutality are quite permissible if the acts are condoned by self–serving religion and conservative, order–loving, self-righteous citizens. The world must beware the callous power of petty officialdom.

Red Noses was also written in 1978 but was not produced until 1985. It is blatantly revolutionary. Medieval corpse bearers, workers forced to pick up and dispose of the bodies of those who died from the Black Death in the fourteenth century, decide to spread the deadly plague as a way of destroying the society that so cruelly exploits them.

Sunset and Glories (1990) is about the short reign of a good pope, St. Celestine, a former monk who fights for the poor. In this play, Barnes came to believe that there is the potential for good in humanity after all.

In *Dreaming* (1999), the bones of slaughtered people are seen under the glass floor of the stage as a tattered band leaves the field of the Battle of Tewkesbury in 1471 during the War of the Roses. Masses of peasants have been butchered and now a symbolic group of survivors are killed one at a time. The hero who opposes the tyrant Richard III finds his loved ones murdered, and he comes to realize that history cannot be rewritten. Still, there is hope because the dead speak of it in farewell, and Christ comes down from the cross to join with the dead. Barnes remains convinced that although genocide continues and cruelty abounds, humans are potentially redeemable.

M A J O R   P L A Y

The Ruling Class (1968)

The Ruling Class is both a melodrama and a farce set in Victorian England. Jack, a paranoid schizophrenic, inherits an earldom as the fourteenth Earl of Gurney. He wears a monk's habit and believes that he is Jesus. With his lurid sexual fantasies, the mad protagonist is surely the end of an aristocratic line. In the prologue, his predecessor, the thirteenth earl, a judge, accidentally hangs himself on a makeshift gallows during a grotesque sadomasochistic rite.

At a key point in the play, Jack's family and the psychiatrist-like Master of Lunacy believe that Jack is cured after violent shock treatments when he gives up his fantasy costume and his blasphemous belief and dons the garb of an upper-class Victorian gentleman complete with right-wing political values: the need for sexual propriety among the lower classes, flogging, and capital punishment for most crimes. But in fact he is degenerating into the most famous of all Victorian murderers, the misogynistic Jack the Ripper.

Then the earl is seen pretending to be an actor on the stage, playing Shakespeare's villainous king, the hunchback Richard III. Jack drags himself into the House of Lords, a space filled with dummies (literally) representing moldering corpses, to speak on the resumption of hanging–according to him, the bond that holds society together–while his hands are dripping with the blood of Claire, his slaughtered wife. The earl's estate eventually comes into the possession of a communist butler. Barnes implies that good and evil cannot be distinguished one from the other. The ruling class cannot be restrained in their privileged lives because they are beyond justice and the power of the law.

Additional Reading

Barnes, Peter. *Collected Plays*. London: Heinemann, 1981.

Dukore, Bernard F. *The Theatre of Peter Barnes*. London: Heinemann, 1981.

——. *Barnstorm: The Plays of Peter Barnes*. New York: Garland, 1995.

Arnold Wesker (1932–)

Arnold Wesker established his reputation as a significant dramatist with the success of three plays now typically referred to as the Wesker triolgy: *Chicken Soup with Barley* (1958), *Roots* (1959), and *I'm Talking about Jerusalem* (1960). The trilogy charts the history of a London East End working–class Jewish family from 1936 to 1959. *Chips with Everything* (1962) confirmed the legitimacy of Wesker's success. The play uses the training of Royal Air Force recruits to discuss the damage class divisions and hierarchical power structures do to individualism as officers attempt to dehumanize the work force.

Wesker is a writer committed to social progress and trade unionism, although in his later years his working–class and liberal allies deserted him, and he became disillusioned. Thus Wesker's early successes did not continue, and as the British public became more conservative, it shied away from his stridency.

Wesker was born in Stepney, East End London. His father was a Jewish tailor who had emigrated from Russia to Britain, and his mother had come from Hungary. She augmented the family's meager income by working in kitchens. During World War II, Wesker was evacuated to several locations in England and Wales along with tens of thousands of other children to keep them safe from the German bombs dropping on London. Wesker was educated at Upton House Technical School, Hackney, London. He left school at sixteen and held various jobs. From 1950 to 1952 he did his required military service in the Royal Air Force. After the RAF, Wesker went back to low–paying jobs while saving money to enter the London School of Film Technique in 1956 where he studied for a year.

Early on, Wesker became interested in writing and the theater. In 1956 the producer Lindsay Anderson read two of Wesker's plays–*The Kitchen* and *Chicken Soup with Barley*–and brought the plays to George Devine of the Royal Court Theatre. A reward from the Arts Council of Great Britain was followed by a production of *Chicken Soup with Barley* in 1958. However,

Chips with Everything (1962) was Wesker's first West End success. Wesker has written radio and television dramas as well as short stories. His plays have tended to have greater success outside of Britain. In 1985 he was elected a Fellow of the Royal Society of Literature.

Wesker married Doreen Bicker in 1958. They have four children.

The Kitchen was first performed in 1959, but was written sometime before *Chicken Soup with Barley*. It is a partly autobiographical work, as Wesker had once worked in the kitchen of a Hungarian restaurant. The restaurant setting is a microcosm of the world. People from several nations work there and eat there. In true capitalist fashion, the owner of the restaurant callously responds to the discontent of his workers by informing them that they must accept that their lives are mainly about hard work.

Their Very Own and Golden City (1965) portrays an architect, Andy Cobham, torn between his ambition and his sense of integrity. After he compromises, both he and the audience feel profoundly defeated. *The Four Seasons* (1965) was not well received. The story of two lovers, Adam and Beatrice, is told in four segments. Beatrice is silent during most of the play and the audience waits for her to speak. They are disappointed when she does, however, for only banalities emerge. The lovers seem to relate best when making apple strudel. In *The Friends* (1970) a woman named Esther is slowly dying of leukemia. Her friends, brother, and lover gather around her bed and carry on their conversations and their lives while forgetting what Esther is going through. Wesker is reminding us of our selfishness, insensitivity, and ability to compartmentalize our feelings.

Jewish subjects, themes, and values structure many of Wesker's plays. *The Old Ones* (1972) is a dark Jewish comedy set in the familiar Wesker territory of London's East End. Unlike several other of Wesker's later plays, it ends in hope and a victory for the defeated as he shows how downtrodden people are worthy not only of sympathy but of respect. *The Merchant* (1976) is a literary play as well as a commentary on anti-Semitism in which Wesker offers his response to the portrayal of Shylock in Shakespeare's *Merchant of Venice*.

Caritas (1981) is set in the fourteenth century. It links politics and religion. Christine Carpenter desires to become an anchoress and isolate herself from the world in religious seclusion. Meanwhile her lover, Robert, is killed in Wat Tyler's peasant rebellion of 1381. He has chosen action in defense of the poor, while Christine hides from the world. Wesker is critical of self-denial and overzealous religiosity.

Blood Libel (1996) is based on the calumny that Jews slew the twelve-year-old William of Norwich in the medieval period to use his blood in a religious ceremony, a rumor that resulted in the pillaging, rape, and murder of the Jews of the Norwich Jewish community. The church is held responsible for instigating the pogrom. *When God Wanted a Son* (1997) was written in 1986 but was not produced until 1997. It portrays a failing mixed marriage between a Jewish professor and his anti-Semitic Anglo-Saxon wife. It is only their daughter who understands that the brutish people of the world murder the gifted whenever they can.

M A J O R   P L A Y S

Chicken Soup with Barley (1958)
Chicken Soup with Barley is the story of the Kahn family, who live in Wesker's East End of London. Sarah and Harry have two children: the teenager Ada and the child Ronnie. The parents are Jews who have emigrated from Hungary to Britain and they are communists. Harry is a timid man, but Sarah has energy and conviction. In October 1936 they join in the breaking up of

a Fascist march. In 1946, undernourished and exhausted by the war that has just ended, they have aged, lost zeal, and do not have much hope for the future.

Then Harry has a stroke. The play turns to the mid–1950s. The British Left has been demoralized by the truth about Stalin's dictatorship and the brutal Soviet suppression of the Hungarian Revolution of 1956. Ronnie, the most upbeat of the family, has lost faith in the future. Only Sarah still has hope for coming days. A neighbor brings the traditional Jewish cure for everything–chicken soup–for Ada when she is sick. That symbolizes for Sarah what life is truly all about–people caring for people.

Roots (1959)

Roots introduces another British family in the trilogy to contrast with the Kahns, a nonpolitical farm family from Norwich. Beatie, the daughter of the family, has fallen in love with Ronnie while living and working in London. She saw the spark of idealism in him and she admired and cherished it. She has returned home to her parents for two weeks, and she realizes how dull rural life now is for her. She mouths Ronnie's values and ideas at first, and then on her own she verbally battles with her mother over the fact that her parents have no ideals and they let the capitalist world exploit them without protest. The family is not convinced nor do they really respect Beatie, but she has become a thinking person and is proud of it. Although Ronnie writes to break off their engagement, Beatie has transformed herself into a woman with a mind of her own and a future that is bright.

I'm Talking about Jerusalem (1960)

I'm Talking about Jerusalem encompasses the years 1946 to 1959. Ada has married. Dave, her husband, fought for the Republic in the Spanish Civil War, and in World War II he served in the Far East. Dave is a skilled furniture maker. The couple lives in a country cottage where Dave pursues his craft in an environment somewhat similar to life in preindustrial Britain, but he really cannot make a decent living because relatively few people want to, or can, spend the money to buy hand-crafted furniture. A life replicating the Arts and Crafts movement of the late Victorian era has no future in post–World War II Britain. Therefore, Ada and Dave give up the shop and the cottage and move to London. It is not really a defeat. They have tried to live by their principles and values.

In the Wesker trilogy the author has sketched Jewish socialist life from the fearful, fascistically inclined 1930s to the reawakening of British conservatism a generation later.

Additional Reading

Dornan, Reade W. *Arnold Wesker Revisited*. New York: Twayne/Macmillan, 1994.

Leeming, Gloria. *Wesker: The Playwright*. London: Methuen, 1982.

Wilcher, Robert. *Understanding Arnold Wesker*. Columbia: University of South Carolina Press, 1991.

Wesker, Arnold. *Plays*. London: Methuen, 2001.

Joe Orton (1933–1967)

Although Joe Orton was not an innovator in the area of dramatic structure, and his fascination with farcical situations came at the expense of characterization, he had a great ability to shock and outrage an audience, especially a middle-class, heterosexual one. Furthermore, his dark comedies effectively exuded an aura of menace that he surely learned from Pinter. With purposeful incongruity to his wild action, Orton's dialogue is often precise and elegant. The term Ortonesque has come to mean a piece of dialogue in which characters say one thing but act fiendishly in opposition to what they have mouthed. In Orton's dramas promiscuity, homosexuality, and perversity are the norms of human behavior. Orton is early "queer"; that is, he flaunts his own sexuality in the face of the audience and demands not only their attention but also their recognition of his truths.

Joe Orton was born in Leicester in a public housing project. He was the eldest child of William and Elizabeth Bentley Orton. Elizabeth worked as a machinist in a factory and William was a gardener. The Ortons were a respectable family that barely got by financially. They were the kind of a family Orton ripped and parodied in his comic satires.

Orton was a sickly child who preferred reading to sports. He often missed school days and he did not make it into an academic high school. Instead he enrolled in a private secretarial school and went to work at the age of sixteen, but lost job after job because of disinterest. Meanwhile he acted in amateur productions and took speech lessons until he was accepted into the Royal Academy of Dramatic Art in London. At the academy, he met Kenneth Halliwell with whom he entered into a writing partnership and a gay marriage that would last for both their short lifetimes. Halliwell, six years older than Orton and well-educated, began to mentor his young and attractive partner.

Orton considered his training at RADA to be of little value, although he remained there from 1950 to 1953. After six months in repertory, Orton abandoned acting. Halliwell and Orton collaborated on several novels, none of which were accepted for publication. In 1962 the pair were arrested and sentenced to six months imprisonment for stealing and defacing books. In prison Orton came to despise society.

After prison, Orton's luck changed. The BBC accepted a

play for radio. In May 1964, *Entertaining Mr Sloane*, Orton's first stage play, opened in London's West End and was a notorious success.

Orton had three exciting years of celebrity and success until the night of August 9, 1967, when Halliwell smashed his partner's skull with nine blows of a hammer and then took his own life with an overdose of barbiturates. Orton died like a character in an Orton play.

Entertaining Mr Sloane (1964) is a play about a psychopath who comes to live with a middle-aged woman and her aggressive, gay brother. After he murders the father of the pair, he is forced to be their sex slave, for they are even more ruthless than he is. The world of *Entertaining Mr Sloane* is one of brutality, exploitation, cruelty, and sadism. That is what lurks behind the doors in the houses of the "respectable" middle class.

Loot (1965) employs the format of a thriller. A dead woman is in a casket. Her husband is under assault from the nymphomaniac, six-times-married nurse, who has in fact murdered his wife. His bank robber son does not much care what is going on for he is engaged with his gay partner. A comic policeman sorts things out. Family values, police, and the medical profession are whipped savagely. *Good and Faithful Servant* (1967) is Orton's most compassionate play. It deals with an old man put out of work by the company he has worked for for fifty years and must now go on welfare. The play is Orton's most political drama, a Marxist indictment of British capitalism.

Orton's last play, *What the Butler Saw* (1969), produced posthumously, is wickedly funny. The institution under attack is the mental hospital where the administrators are the lunatics. Orton's dramatic world is full of the mad or near-mad as well as fools and connivers doomed to be hoisted on their own petards.

Entertaining Mr Sloane (1964)

Joe Orton delighted in turning both the conventions of the traditional family and the usual expectations in sexual relations upside down and inside out in this play about murder, blackmail, and sex. Sloane, an amoral young man, and Kath, a frumpy middle-aged woman who wants to mother and have "incestuous" sex with Sloane, share her apartment. Her gay misogynist brother, Ed, arrives and becomes the dominant male. He wants Sloane to be his chauffeur and come live with him. When Ed learns that Sloane and Kath have been having sex together he is furious.

Ironically, Sloane the murderer becomes the play's victim. Having beaten Kath's and Ed's Dadda to death to prevent being arrested for murdering the father's employer, Sloane becomes the prisoner of the siblings, and he cannot protest when they decide that he will be their mutual sex slave. Sloane can be taken to be symbolically the incestuous child of Ed and Kath.

Loot (1965)

A gay couple, Harold McLeavy and his partner Dennis, have stolen money from a bank, and they have hidden it in Harold's mother's coffin, which is on stage. In front of the casket, Harold's father receives the sexual attentions of Nurse Kay. An odd policeman named Truscott, pretending to be from the Water Board, is investigating a possible murder, and he gets Kay, who has had six husbands so far, to confess to brutally murdering Mrs. McLeavy. She had been jealous of the woman she murdered, and frustrated because she is childless despite her many sexual partners.

The young men engage in sadomasochistic sex. The policeman, representing societal morality, is comic, thus implying that the outside world really cannot control what individuals do with or to each other in their private lives. Orton treats comically a situation that is basically tragic and, of course, trashes the family.

What the Butler Saw (1969)

What the Butler Saw is Orton's best and funniest farce–his masterpiece. It is a madcap play full of sexual reversals. As often happens in farces, a frantic husband is trying to find a dress for a naked woman. A Dr. Rance interprets the actions of the play by diagnosing the remarks of the characters as schizophrenic, which makes them all certifiably mad, and when the plays ends, he leads the befuddled characters through a skylight on the way to an institution.

Set in the clinic of Dr. Prentice (really an apprentice?), the doctor is trying to seduce his new secretary, Geraldine, while supposedly giving her a medical examination. Meanwhile Mrs. Prentice is at a meeting of her lesbian coven, but she returns during the "examination." Prentice must hide the nude Geraldine, and he farcically lies his way out of his problematic situation. Geraldine winds up in the clothes of a hotel porter named Nicholas who has been carrying Mrs. Prentice's bags as well as having sex with her. It turns out that he and Geraldine are twin brother and sister and the children of the Prentices, conceived in the linen closet of a hotel, although no one is aware of the fact until later in the play. Yikes! Incest too!

As in all good farces, the set is full of doors. A statue of Winston Churchill has lost its penis. History is ridiculed. Civilization is crumbling. Chaos and sexual license is celebrated in Orton's carnivalesque world.

Additional Reading
Bigsby, C. W. E. *Joe Orton*. London: Methuen, 1982.

Lahr, John. *Prick Up Your Ears: The Biography of Joe Orton*. New York: Knopf, 1978.

Orton, Joe. *The Complete Plays*. New York: Grove, 1977.

Rusinko, Susan. *Joe Orton*. New York: Twayne, 1995.

David Storey (1933–)

Like D. H. Lawrence, the son of an English North Country miner, David Storey has shown his concern and sympathy for the workers in the region of his birth. As with D. H. Lawrence, Storey's characters speak with an unaffected eloquence and are in touch with the basic passions of life: love, hate, fear, and the search for security. Storey's plays are sensual. His characters are flesh and blood. Storey understands the power of the metaphor on stage as symbol and microcosm: a tent or a locker room may represent a community or society in general. Storey, a former athlete, enjoys "using" the body as he pictures men and women working and washing, and eating and touching. He is ever cognizant of, and usually addressing, the pitfalls of the British class system, which he generally examines from the working-class perspective, the class he most admires.

David Storey is a rare writer: one who has had a successful career as a playwright and a novelist. His most successful novel, *This Sporting Life* (1960), is a brilliant study of the passions of a working-class athlete in the north of England. It won several awards and the film version in 1963 is recognized as a masterpiece of British cinema.

David Malcolm Storey was born in Wakefield in the coal fields of Yorkshire. He was educated at the Queen Elizabeth Grammar School in Wakefield from 1943 to 1951, the Wakefield College of Art from 1951 to 1953, and the Slade School of Fine Art from 1953 to 1956, where he studied painting and from which he received a diploma in fine arts in 1956.

Storey was a professional rugby player for the Leeds Rugby League Club from 1952 to 1956. He married Barbara Rudd Hamilton in 1956. The couple has four children. David Storey has written ten novels.

The Restoration of Arnold Middleton (1967), Storey's first play, was a major success. It is about a neurotic man rebelling against the confinement of middle–class suburban life. *In Celebration* (1969) takes place during a fortieth wedding anniversary party at which a son who has left his working–class home and relatives in order to do better in the world returns home and causes fireworks as family wounds are exposed.

The Contractor (1970) centers on the erection and dismantling of a marquee, a large open–sided tent, for a wedding reception. It celebrates the satisfactions of manual labor while the contractor works out his relationship with his university-educated son. It also features the conflict between English and Irish workers. *Home* (1970) treats the illusions and realities of life in a mental institution where inmates find psychological confrontation unbearable. *The Changing Room* (1971) presents the interaction of a rugby team–the owners, managers, players, and trainers–before, during, and after a match. It is about the combat of sport and the hopes and ambitions of the young gladiators. *Cromwell* (1973) presents both sides of England's civil war. *The Farm* (1973) is an anatomy of a large family of a hard–drinking farmer. *Life Class* (1974) is set in an art college, and it discusses the several motivations of art students.

After *Life Class*, Storey's popularity declined and most of his later plays were unsuccessful. *Mother's Day* (1976), ironically titled, is a comedy about the battles of a housepainter's family living in a public housing complex. *Sisters* (1978) is also set in a housing estate, where a prostitution racket is run by a former professional football player and his wife. The wife's sister arrives and becomes involved in the family business. In *Early Days* (1980), an elderly gentleman of some accomplishment is deemed by his daughter and his servants to be unable to take care of himself. *The March on Russia* (1989) is a sequel to *In Celebration*. Alas, in the later play, youth and hope have been lost.

MAJOR PLAY

Home (1970)

Home is a very subtle play of character. Its precise dialogue is almost musical. In a home for mental patients, men and women carry on a conversation. Two older men, Harry and Jack, are flirtatious with the women, trying to impress them and each other. They are well dressed and seem healthy. They talk of politics, important acquaintances, the adventures of their earlier lives, and World War II. They want and need to be seen and respected as retired gentlemen of the world. Their conversation, however, is full of clichés. Albert, a younger man, tries to impress the women with his physical strength, but that seems immature to them. The women are incredulous and not impressed with the men. In the second act they are a demolition squad, blowing up male pretensions.

Marjorie and Kathleen are realistic about their positions. Marjorie, a working-class woman, is glad she is institutionalized. This home is better for her than the home she left. The women enjoy their bawdiness and vulgarity. Men are really quite funny to them. They want to know what the men are in for. Clearly, women are better prepared to face the vicissitudes of life. They can survive and thrive in dire circumstances. Men cannot. In the end Harry and Jack, feeling defeated and humiliated, break down in tears.

Additional Reading

Hutchings, William. *The Plays of David Storey: A Thematic Study.* Carbondale: Southern Illinois University Press, 1988.

Liebman, Herbert. *The Dramatic Art of David Storey: The Journey of a Playwright.* Westport, Conn.: Greenwood, 1996.

Storey, David. *Plays: One.* London: Methuen, 1992.

———. *Plays: Two.* London: Methuen, 1994.

Michael Frayn (1933–)

Michael Frayn is an award-winning novelist, a journalist, a translator of Russian and French literature, and, most of all, a cerebral playwright whose plays range from uproarious farces to philosophical and moral discourses. Frayn likes to deal with society in terms of the institutions that control our lives: industry, the news media, government, and the scientific establishment. Frayn's farces always show a tragic possibility peeking and grimacing from beneath the skirt of comedy. He shows us the madness of everyday life. But he also can connect us to the most profound moral questions of our time.

Michael Frayn was born in north London. His father was a sales representative for a manufacturing company and his mother took care of the home. The family moved to Ewell in Surrey not long after Frayn was born. When Frayn's mother died, his father, unable to pay for a housekeeper and Frayn's private school–Sutton High School for Boys–transferred his son to the Kingston Grammar School, where Frayn was not an outstanding scholar. Upon leaving school, Frayn commenced his mandatory national service in 1952, first as a medical corpsman in the Royal Artillery and then in the Intelligence Corps.

When he left the army in 1954, Frayn entered Emmanuel

College, Cambridge, first majoring in French and Russian and then switching to philosophy. He received the bachelor of arts degree in 1957 and went to work for the *Manchester Guardian*, first as a general reporter and then as a columnist. He left the *Guardian* in 1962 and went to work for the *London Observer* until 1968, when he began earning enough money from the publication of his early novels to be able to live off his writing.

Frayn married Gillian Palmer in 1960. The couple had three children. The marriage was dissolved in 1990. Frayn is now married to the award-winning biographer Claire Tomalin.

Alphabetical Order (1975) is set in a newspaper library, the "morgue" that is inundated with copies and clippings. A well-meaning librarian cannot order or control the room even when she leads others in taking over the newspaper that has been producing the flood of trivia. In *Donkeys' Years* (1976), a college reunion, always good for farcical treatment, turns into a rowdy and revealing bacchanal. *Clouds* (1976) is a comedy about a press junket to Cuba in which Frayn argues that the clouds are a good metaphor for the way political perceptions shift. In *Liberty Hall* (1979), Balmoral Castle, the Scotland residence of Queen Elizabeth II, is invaded and taken over by a writers' collective in the way that the Bolsheviks took over the Winter Palace in St. Petersburg in 1917.

Benefactors (1964) explores the kinds of intimacies and dependencies two friendly couples can get into. *Noises Off* (1982) is an unusual example of a genre parodying a genre. In this case, a company putting on a play called *Nothing On* is made fun of by showing what disasters are happening in front of and behind the curtain. *Look Look* (1990) returns to the theater as a subject. Now an onstage audience seems to be watching the actual audience, who come to realize that the onstage audience is watching a play within a play. Frayn is saying "look again" at the illusion of the theater.

Now You Know (1995) concerns a government cover-up of police brutality and the secret prejudices all people have. *Copenhagen* (1998), an intellectual masterpiece, is about the moral responsibility of scientists when science has the capacity to destroy the world. Not unrelated to the themes in *Copenhagen*, *Alarms and Excursions* (1998) speaks of the dehumanization of life by technology. *Democracy* (2003) depicts the complications of the 1974 spy scandal that forced Willy Brandt to resign as chancellor of West Germany. The theatergoing public wonders which will be Frayn's future direction: farce or the morality play?

MAJOR   PLAYS

Noises Off (1982)

Noises Off is a brilliantly and precisely orchestrated backstage farce. Its operative subject is the often creaky mechanics of theater. In the play, a sex farce called *Nothing On*, by one Robin Housemonger, is being rehearsed rather badly. The actress Doty Otley is playing a housekeeper. She is a television star in need of a stage vehicle to make some money because her TV career is fading. In fact she is backing the show as an investment. Doty can handle neither lines nor props. Furthermore she is having an affair with the young leading man who is playing a real estate agent. The director is chasing both the sexy ingénue and the assistant stage manager, Poppy. Disaster must ensue and it does in the second act, which takes place backstage while *Nothing On* is being performed. We see the actors rushing through entrances to the unseen stage and audience. They hit each other and fall down. The stage manager must go on as a replacement. Finally the actors themselves drag the curtain down to separate themselves from the silent, but presumably stunned, unseen audience.

As the play and the play within the play crash to a close,

Poppy shouts out that she is pregnant. Hysteria has ruled supreme, and we realize through our tears of laughter that theatrical farce is a superb metaphor for life.

Copenhagen (1998)

Copenhagen is a play of ideas that requires deep intellectual concentration on the part of the audience. It takes place in September 1941 in German-occupied Copenhagen at the home of the brilliant nuclear physicist Neils Bohr. His equally brilliant former student, Werner Heisenberg, pays Bohr an unexpected visit. Heisenberg developed the famous uncertainty principle, which states that a particle under observation changes as a direct result of being observed, and therefore the results of observations are inevitably uncertain. Heisenberg has been working for Hitler to produce a German atom bomb, which could win the war for the Nazis, but he may be trying, as he hints, to delay the project.

Bohr, who has a Jewish wife and is thus vulnerable, is not certain what Heisenberg really wants. He is observing his former student, who is observing him, perhaps to see if he is in touch with Allied nuclear physicists. Heisenberg is, after all, the head of the German nuclear project, and if he is not trying to pump Bohr for information about Allied nuclear progress, he is trying to protect himself from postwar prosecution if Germany should lose, by giving the impression that he is traitorously delaying the project. Or Heisenberg may really be delaying the project knowing that the German cause is the evil one. Another possibility is that Heisenberg may be trying to get his admired mentor to make the choice for him. And on, and on.

Nothing is concluded. Heisenberg goes back to Germany and the atom bomb project. Neither man has seen into the other's heart: the truth of the human soul, like the wandering

of an electron, is indeterminable, and depends on who is looking into it.

Additional Reading
Frayn, Michael. *Copenhagen.* New York: Anchor, 1998.
——. *Noises Off.* London: Methuen, 1983.

Edward Bond (1934–)

Edward Bond is a moralist. He believes human actions always
have consequences, and that dictum applies to playwrights and
their work. Bond is angered at those who profess art for art's
sake; he believes the artist's mind, heart, and gut must serve
humanity. Bond reports that violence is just another cheap
commodity in capitalism. His Brechtian agitprop and overt socialism went out of fashion when Britain turned to the right in
the 1970s and 1980s, but Bond will not be forgotten. His violent
stage imagery and his attack on capitalistic greed and exploitation will continue to inspire young playwrights with fire in
them.

Thomas Edward Bond was born in Holloway, north London, the son of a laborer from East Anglia who had brought his
family to London to find work in the depression. During World
War II, Bond was evacuated to East Anglia to live with his
grandparents. He was educated at Crouch End Secondary
Modern School, where a performance of *Macbeth* stoked his interest in theater. Leaving school at fifteen, he took a series of
menial jobs and did national service in the army from 1953 to
1955. Bond wrote more than a dozen plays before *The Pope's Wedding* was produced at the Royal Court Theatre in 1962, and he
was able to write full-time for the theater. In 1971 Bond married
Elisabeth Pablé. Bond has also written screenplays and poetry.

The Pope's Wedding (1962) tells the story of a young man,

Scopey, who performs brilliantly at a cricket match, whereupon he impresses a girl and marries her. Scopey meets and becomes obsessed with a recluse. He loses his job, his marriage fails, and he murders the hermit. Life had neither point nor purpose for him after the glory of the cricket match.

Saved (1965) is a powerful evocation of urban violence that was banned by the lord chamberlain, the British censor. In *Narrow Road to the Deep North* (1968), Bond deals with the mechanics of oppression that lead to political justification of the murder of children. *Early Morning* (1969), banned by the lord chamberlain for political reasons, caricatures Queen Victoria, Prince Albert, and Florence Nightingale as oppressors and exploiters of the people.

Lear (1971) is Bond's Brechtian version of Shakespeare's play, in which he emphasizes the ferocity and cruelty in the original. Bond's Lear is a greater–than–life and highly symbolic figure, but then, so is Shakespeare's. In the end of Bond's play, the old man, who has brought unremitting violence into the world, is pitifully trying to dig up his great wall, the symbol of the failed social order he tried to create.

Bingo (1973), a biographical portrait of the last, sad days of Shakespeare's life, is a powerful polemic on the responsibility of the artist in society. In *The Sea* (1973), the protagonist comes to realize how little death means to other humans. *The Fool* (1975) is based on the life of John Clare, an early–nineteenth-century working–class poet who went mad. Bond implies in *The Woman* (1978) that a wealthy, materialistic, exploiting state that is devoid of spiritual values would benefit from an armed insurrection.

In *The Bundle* (1978) a contemplative man gives up his otherworldly contemplation to become a wealthy capitalist, and thus sows the seeds of his own well–earned destruction. Violence is the way to utopia. *The Worlds* (1979) has striking workers refusing to return to work in order to save their kidnapped boss. In this play, Bond justifies terrorism when it is used against capitalistic oppression.

Restoration (1981) is a Brechtian play of history and revolution accompanied by songs. It is based on *The Relapse*, a Restoration-era comedy by John Vanbrugh. In *Summer* (1982), a woman who has participated in fascist atrocities in the Balkans during World War II is cast as the embodiment of villainy. *The War Plays* (1985) implies that even a nuclear holocaust would serve the cause of world revolution.

In his 1996 play *In the Company of Men*, Bond argues that extremism is a reasonable response to a desperate situation that could lead to annihilation. *Coffee* (1997) confused the audience by its juxtaposing the 1941 massacre of thirty thousand Jews by the SS at Babi Yar with the fading away of small villages in Wales.

MAJOR   PLAYS

Saved (1965)

Saved is a morality tale about the good in a human being struggling to save the individual. The protagonist, Len, has a one-night stand with Pam. Then she finds that she is pregnant, and they move in with her parents. After the baby is born, Pam is quickly bored with Len and with the child, whom she neglects shamelessly. The main family activity is watching television. Len is unsure of himself. He even puts up with Pam's affair with a new boyfriend. Psychologically regressing, Len adopts an Oedipal relationship with Pam's willing mother.

Len then bonds with four other young men who meet in a park to tell sexual jokes and denigrate women. In fact they are afraid of women. The men are like a primitive tribe looking for sex, sadistic opportunities, and violence. Finally, the brutal world closes in as Len's pals stone the baby to death in its carriage while Len looks on and does nothing. The death of an innocent in such a fashion is Bond's indictment of humanity. But Len does achieve redemption. At the end of the play, he is seen fixing a chair. It is a small start on something constructive in his life. Work is the way to salvation. Still, outside any door anarchy and brutality reign.

It should be noted that Bond has been faulted by feminist critics who find that, with few exceptions, his moral questions are centered on male characters.

Bingo (1973)

From his school days on, Bond has been fascinated with Shakespeare. In *Bingo*, Bond's masterpiece, the author reconstructs Shakespeare's last days in Stratford. In a brilliant reproduction of life in a small Jacobean Midlands market town, Bond portrays Shakespeare betraying his fellow villagers by signing away their rights to the people's traditional common pasture. Shakespeare is more the antisocial criminal because he is a genius. Art cannot, must not, be separated from life. Creativity and brilliance bring responsibilities, and not just to art. Shakespeare cannot reconcile the humanistic values he professed in his drama with his acquisitive self and his complicity in a social order that is patently unjust. Thus he takes his own life.

Additional Reading

Bond, Edward. *The Hidden Plot: Notes on the Theatre and the State*. London: Methuen, 2000.
——. *Plays*. London: Methuen, 1977.
——. *Plays: Two*. London: Methuen, 1978.
——. *Plays: Five*. London: Methuen Drama, 1996.
Coult, Tony. *The Plays of Edward Bond*. London: Methuen, 1977.

Hirst, David L. *Edward Bond.* Basingstoke: Macmillan, 1985.

Scharine, Richard G. *The Plays of Edward Bond.* Lewisburg, Pa.: Bucknell University Press, 1976.

Alan Bennett (1934–)

The world of Alan Bennett's drama is a small world inhabited by small people; even when the characters represent important political or historical figures, they are small. But out of incidents come insights into human nature, laughter, and some instructive self-awareness for the audience. His fine ear for natural dialogue greatly enhances the pleasures derived from Bennett's satires and farces.

Alan Bennett was born in Leeds, Yorkshire. His father was a butcher and his mother was a homemaker. He was educated at Leeds Modern School from 1946 to 1952, after which he did his mandatory national service at the Joint Services School for Linguistics from 1952 to 1954, followed by Exeter College, Oxford, from 1954 to 1957, receiving the bachelor of arts degree with honors in 1957. Bennett was a junior lecturer at Oxford's Magdalen College from 1960 to 1962, after which he commenced a television writing and performing career that eventually led to the stage. But first Bennett was brilliant in television. In the 1960s, the satirical review *Beyond the Fringe* made him a star of comedy alongside Jonathan Miller, Dudley Moore, and Peter Cooke. *Talking Heads* (1987), monologues originally written for television, has also had success on the stage.

As a playwright, Bennett continues to evolve, but some themes and characters persist. He espouses sexual freedom and is disenchanted with the British political scene and the way the welfare state has provided for the body but not the soul. He likes to lampoon the royal family. He is intrigued by spies. The

Jewish–Czech modernist writer Franz Kafka, master of quiet terror, fascinates Bennett and appears in two plays: *Kafka's Dick* and the television play *The Insurance Man*, both of 1986. Bennett, a farce lover who is not a misogynist, often places a wise, intelligent, and wryly funny woman at the center of his plays. She is a point-of-view character, and the teller of truth.

The sketch-filled satire *Forty Years On* (1968) brought Bennett success in a new medium: the theater. It is a hail and farewell to the charm and the glow of the long-faded Edwardian age as well as a send-up of public school life and the Bloomsbury group. The play is full of delightfully wicked sketches of cultural idols like Oscar Wilde and Virginia Woolf. *Getting On* (1971) is about a Labour Party member of Parliament, George Oliver, who cannot comprehend contemporary political and sexual realities. He finds it hard to serve his West Indian constituents, and he is stunned by the fact that his son by his first wife, his young second wife, and a gay Conservative Party MP have formed an unconventional triangle.

The farce *Habeas Corpus* (1973) portrays a physician, a general practitioner, who is quite disillusioned by the human body but yet, in a good old-fashioned farce about lechery, pursues a well-built young woman patient. *The Old Country* (1978) shows the life of the former spy Guy Burgess, who escaped to the Soviet Union and who tries to recreate the life he and his wife left behind when they fled England. *Enjoy* (1980) depicts a North England family awaiting the demolition of their home and wondering where they will go. The daughter is a prostitute of whom the parents are quite proud. The other child is a transsexual social worker. The play mocks social planners and the idea that in human affairs one size can fit all.

The Madness of George III (1991) is a masterful humanization of the king who lost the American colonies for Great Britain. *A Question of Attribution* (1998) interweaves an intellectual discussion on the authenticity of art with contemporary politics. It discusses the treachery of the art historian and spy Sir Anthony Blunt.

M A J O R   P L A Y

The Madness of George III (1991)

In *The Madness of George III*, the dramatist blends his knowledge of Shakespeare's history plays and *King Lear* with a study of eighteenth-century politics and the treatment of the mentally ill. George is an engaging, human, and magnificently constructed character who, like Lear, is "bound upon a wheel of fire." The fire is his mental illness. But it is also the torture inflicted on him by the doctors and the humiliation of having his unpleasant symptoms announced to the country. King George is an innocent, subject to the manipulations of counselors and physicians. He is a loving husband and father who is not well prepared to lead in the complex society of eighteenth-century Britain. George has our sympathy. The great surprise of the drama is that the king recovers from his second bout of madness and dismisses his brutally controlling doctors, so the play ends happily with George in control of his realm and his life.

The Madness of George III is obviously not a tragedy, and thus we can more easily relate to the ordinariness of a gentle king. Like the play, the film version, entitled *The Madness of King George*, was a major international success.

Additional Reading

Bennett, Alan. *Plays: One*. London: Faber and Faber, 1996.

——. *Plays: Two*. London: Faber and Faber, 1998.

O'Mealy, Joseph H. *Alan Bennett: A Critical Introduction*. New York: Routledge, 2001.

Wolfe, Peter. *Understanding Alan Bennett*. Columbia: University of South Carolina Press, 1999.

Trevor Griffiths (1935–)

Trevor Griffiths is a Marxist playwright whose great desire has been to see significant social change in British society. He has moved many audiences without harangues. His main theme is the uphill struggle of the proletariat, especially the workers in the British Midlands of his birth, childhood, youth, and education. Except for *The Gulf between Us* (1992), a reaction to the Gulf War of 1991, Griffiths's dramatic writing for the last twenty or so years has been for television. This has caused the playwright to be accused by critics on the left of selling out, since he advocates radical societal changes but has a bourgeois career. But Griffith's body of work, both for the stage and television, is a manifesto of his deep concern for, and commitment to, humanity.

Trevor Griffiths was born in Manchester, Lancashire, where he attended St. Bede's College from 1945 to 1952 and the University of Manchester from 1952 to 1955, receiving a bachelor of arts degree in English. He undertook national service as an infantryman in the Manchester Regiment of the British Army from 1955 to 1957. After leaving the service, Griffiths taught school in Oldham, Lancashire, from 1957 to 1961, and was a lecturer at the Stockport Technical College, Cheshire, from 1962 to 1965. Griffiths coedited *Labour's Northern Voice* and was a series editor for the Workers Northern Publishing Society. Griffiths has always been committed to the labor union movement.

Griffiths went to work for the BBC in Leeds until success on the stage in 1969 and in television in 1972 allowed him to devote most of his time to writing. Griffiths married Janice Elaine Stansfield in 1960. They had a son and two daughters. Janice died in 1977.

Occupations (1970) is set in Turin, Italy, when the post–World War I revolutionary spirit infused the workers who took over the factories and formed soviets. The conflict is between two approaches to communism: one is idealistic and compassionate, the other is pragmatic. In *The Party* (1973), a group of non–working–class British leftists discuss joint action with the revolutionary forces at the barricades in Paris in 1968. The ruminations of the radical–chic gang get nowhere, as Griffiths savagely satirizes the parlor politics of the educated, establishment leftists. Griffiths's greatest success has been *The Comedians* (1975), an investigation into the role of the stand–up comedian in society.

MAJOR   PLAY

The Comedians (1975)

The Comedians is a disturbing play because it concludes that human beings will never divest themselves of the ignorance that creates prejudices, reinforces stereotypes, and does so much damage to society. *The Comedians* examines the role of the stand–up comic in society. Should the comedian cause audience members to challenge their received values and force them to rethink their prejudices, or should the comedian give audiences what they want: reinforcement of their self–perceived superiority over "others"? This conflict of purpose is expressed through the views of two characters. Bert Challenor, the external examiner for the Manchester night–school class in comedy–the setting for the play–believes that comedy is a market commodity and the comedian should shape the product according to the desires of the consumers. The course instructor, Eddie Waters, sees comedy as a way of challenging the audience's false values and exposing truths. Waters respects the audience; Challenor does not.

The play has three parts: classroom preparation, performances, and the aftermath. Those students who follow Waters's philosophy receive no help from Challenor, while those who corrupt their acts to please the examiner are rewarded with professional contacts. Some performers cannot decide what to do and they fall flat. A student named Price presents a brilliant but ultimately chilling act that shows the class hatred of working-class youths toward the well-educated and well-dressed. The act is designed to make the audience participate in hating themselves. Waters is stunned. There are truths that are too dangerous to be looked into deeply.

Additional Reading

Gardner, Stanton B. *Trevor Griffiths: Politics, Drama, History*. Ann Arbor: University of Michigan Press, 1999.

Griffiths, Trevor. *Plays: One*. London: Faber and Faber, 1996.

John McGrath (1935–)

A socialist playwright, John McGrath tends to set his plays in the past and in Scotland. He wants to show the relationship of people not only to other people but to history. McGrath's purpose is to raise social consciousness. In several ways, his agitprop theater, especially *The Imperial Policeman* (1984), owes much to the precedent set by Joan Littlewood's musical theater productions.

In 1971 McGrath founded the 7:84 Theatre Company to bring socialist drama to the workers, using nontheatrical venues. In the 1970s seven percent of the British population owned eighty-four percent of the nation's wealth: thus the company's name. The company worked primarily in Scotland with an offshoot that toured England.

John Peter McGrath was born in Birkenhead, Cheshire. He

studied at Alun Grammar School in Mold, Wales, prior to national service in the army from 1953 to 1955. McGrath went on
to St. John's College, Oxford, and studied there from 1955 to
1959. He was a farm worker before becoming a play reader for
the Royal Court Theatre in 1959. Television writing and directing followed until the founding of the 7:84 Theatre Company.
McGrath married Elizabeth MacLennan in 1962. The couple has
a daughter and two sons.

Events While Guarding the Bofors Gun (1966), based on
McGrath's army experience, had a small success. The play attacks conscription and the frustration of working with obsolete
equipment to stave off the Soviet hordes. Random Happenings in
the Hebrides (1970) is about seeking social justice through opposition to the British parliament. The Cheviot, the Stag, and the Black,
Black Oil (1973) was written to inform a Scottish audience how
they had been exploited. In The Game's a Bogey (1974), McGrath
focuses on the life of the Scottish socialist leader John McClean.
In Joe's Drum (1979), a determined wife strips away her husband's vanity. John Brown's Body (1990) emphasizes the power
difference between classes by having the ruling class direct
workers and audience from a high platform, like the gods in
Greek tragedy. McGrath has written almost thirty plays, and he
has also written successfully for the screen and television.

Simon Gray (1936–)

Simon Gray is one of the most popular living British playwrights. He has brought great pleasure to two generations of
theatergoers. His output has been enormous. Yet he receives
scant critical attention. Perhaps this is because he has been
seen as a dramatist who writes exclusively for the middle-class
West End audience. This may not be fair. Gray has continually
developed his drama from early, Orton–like, savage farces such

as *Wise Child* (1967) and *Dutch Uncle* (1969) through and beyond comedies of manners like the international success *Quartermaine's Terms* (1981), a classically constructed character play set in a school's faculty room. It tells the story of a gentle, friendly, but unsuccessful English tutor who simply fades away at the end of term.

Gray is the arch playwright of constrained emotion, of holding back, of characters showing little to the world for fear of ridicule, exposure, or the self-realization that one's life has so little to offer. His men are unhappy. They do not like their roles in life. Academics are a favorite subject. Bedroom farces are not ruled out, and Gray writes thrillers too. Always, his dialogue is precise and even elegant. Gray has had his flops, not surprising considering his output, but his many hits have kept him in the forefront of British playwrights.

Simon Gray was born on Hayling Island, Hampshire. His father was a physician who had come from Canada. His early education was in Montreal to which he had been evacuated during World War II. He then attended Westminster School, London. Returning to Canada, Gray studied at Dalhousie University in Halifax, Nova Scotia, from 1954 to 1957. He was awarded the bachelor of arts degree with honors in English in 1957. Returning to England, he studied at Trinity College, Cambridge, from 1958 to 1961, receiving another bachelor of arts degree in English in 1961. Gray remained at Trinity College for a year as a researcher before going to Canada once more as a lecturer in English at the University of British Columbia from 1963 to 1964. Back at Trinity College he was a supervisor in English from 1964 to 1966. He also became an editor of *Delta* magazine in 1964. Gray then settled in a lectureship in English at Queen Mary College, London, for twenty years, long after he had begun his successful playwriting career. Gray remains an honorary fellow of Queen Mary College.

Gray married Beryl Mary Kevern in 1965. They have two children.

Butley (1971) was Gray's first major success. The title character, a teacher, is a homosexual who has married in an attempt to escape his sexuality. He is terribly maladjusted. He snipes at and belittles his wife. After six months of marriage, he leaves his wife to return to his lover, a student of his. But no one can bear Butley's bitter tongue and hatefulness. He tortures people with words. Finally he is so self-hating that he cannot begin another student affair. He has destroyed his own life.

The Rear Column (1978), a savage satire worthy of the pen of Evelyn Waugh, is about the loss of moral judgement. The time is 1887 and a relief expedition of British troops is marching to the rescue of an African pasha. The protagonist, Major Barttelot, and four other white men are left behind with 500 blacks to guard a camp while they are surrounded by thousands of other, hostile Africans. Barttelot becomes more savage than any "savage." He flogs the natives, shoots some, and winds up eating them, too. A British naturalist, left with Barttlelot, also becomes unbalanced. He watches as a black girl is killed, cooked, and eaten in order to be able to sketch the business of cannibalism. So much for enlightened imperialism and the White Man's Burden.

The Common Pursuit: Scenes from Literary Life (1984) is an episodic play about friendship. It depicts the changing fortunes of six Cambridge friends and their literary lives as writers, editors, publishers, and scholars. Also discussed are their marriages, divorces, and career successes and failures. Five are the brightest and the best, and one, less successful, lives through the accomplishments of the others. They hurt each other. They grow apart. The protagonist destroys his own life. The play's title is the same as the title of a major book of criticism by F. R. Leavis, a literary critic Gray much admired.

The Late Middle Class (1999) is Gray's elegy on the sexual cer-
tainties of mid-twentieth-century Britain. *The Old Masters* (2004)
is about the art critic Bernard Berenson and the late 1930s. Gray
has also written four novels and many television plays; the latter have been especially successful.

Additional Reading
Burkman, Katherine H., ed. *Simon Gray: A Casebook.* New York: Garland,
1992.

David Rudkin (1936–)

David Rudkin's uniquely provocative dramas contain such
shockers as guards sodomizing inmates, dismemberment, madness, animal copulation, and cannibalism. His is the night-
mare world of the dark side of the moon. There is no limit to
human cruelty and depravity. His shark attack on society's
norms has, however, caused the marginalization of his work.
Regretably, sensibilities in commercial theater can only be
challenged so far.

David James Rudkin was born in London. His father was an
evangelical pastor and his mother a schoolteacher. Rudkin's
rearing was thoroughly anchored in an atmosphere of puritan-
ical denial of the pleasures of life. He was educated at King Edward's School, Birmingham, from 1947 to 1955. Military service
followed in the Royal Signals Corps from 1955 to 1957. He then
went on to St. Catherine's College, Oxford, from 1957 to 1961.
He received the master of arts degree in 1961. From 1961 to
1964 Rudkin was an assistant master of Greek, Latin, and music
at Country High School, Bromsgrove, Worcestershire. He married Alexandra Margaret Thompson in 1967. The couple has
four children. Rudkin has spent much time in Northern Ireland
and is interested in the ongoing Irish question. He has also

written scenarios and librettos for operas and radio plays for the BBC.

Rudkin had a smash hit with the RSC's production of *Afore Night Come* in 1961. This Artaud-like mythic evocation of blood sacrifice in an orchard in the British Midlands in which an Irish migrant worker is killed still has symbolic significance.

Ashes (1973) uses the failure to conceive a child as a metaphor for a sectarian hatred that can only be seen as a communal death wish. *Cries from Casement as His Bones Are Brought to Dublin* (1974) discusses the politics of sex used as a tool in the British control of Ireland. The play was first written for radio. *The Sons of Light* (1976) is set on a remote Scottish Atlantic island held captive in the grip of a patriarchal, fundamentalist, wrathful religion. *The Triumph of Death* (1981) depicts the perversion of natural life by Christianity in the Middle Ages. Although *The Saxon Shore* (1986) is set in Roman Britain in A.D. 410, it is really a political play concerning modern Northern Ireland. A Saxon community and a displaced Celtic community face each other across Hadrian's Wall while the demoralized and relatively ineffectual Roman (British) legion looks on in frustration. All parties commit atrocities at night in the never-ending cycle of violence.

Additional Reading

Rabey, David Ian. *David Rudkin: Sacred Disobedience: An Expository Study of His Drama, 1959–1996*. Amsterdam, The Netherlands: Harwood Academic Publishers, 1997.

Rudkin, David. *Afore Night Come*. New York: Grove, 1966.

Steven Berkoff (1937–)

In the fateful year of 1968, Steven Berkoff established his own theater organization, the London Theatre Group, to showcase his own satiric plays. Among his goals was to bash taboo barriers, especially those related to speaking about sex. He likes to parody literary and drama classics.

Berkoff especially succeeded in an outrageous characterizing and inventory-taking of female sexual organs in his most notorious and influential play *East* (1975). Berkoff found the way to political statement in the body and physicality. Berkoff has had a strong influence on contemporary experimental and political fringe productions.

Berkoff was born in London's East End and schooled first in Stepney and then at Hackney Downs Grammar School, London. Further education included the Webber-Douglas Academy of Dramatic Art in London from 1958 to 1959 and École Jacque Lecoq in Paris in 1965. Berkoff worked in repertory theater for six years before the founding of the London Theatre Group.

Based on the experiences of Berkoff's youth, *East* is a story of growing up in London's East End where young men fornicate and fight. Two friends, Mike and Les, explain to the audience how they were ready to kill each other when they first met. They fought over Mike's girlfriend, Sylv. The fight is described as well as the trip to the hospital. They then become pals over mutual hatred of Sylv, who wishes she had been born a man. They have sexual freedom; she does not. Monologue follows monologue. Mum relates her experience in a cinema where she engaged in mutual masturbation with a stranger only to realize when the lights went on that he was her son. The men in the play are angry. They have low self-confidence and self-esteem. Consequently, they are ready to lash out at society.

West (1983) is based on the legend of Beowulf. *Sink the Belgrano!* (1986) is a parody of Shakespeare's *Henry V*. Later plays include *Kvetch* (1987); *Massage* (1997); *Acapulco* (1994), a send-up of

Hollywood; and *Shakespeare's Villains* (1998), a Shakespearean parody.

Additional Reading
Berkoff, Steven. *Plays: One*. London: Faber and Faber, 2000.
—— and Roger Morton. *The Theatre of Steven Berkoff*. London: Methuen Drama, 1992.

Tom Stoppard (1937–)

Tom Stoppard, like Harold Pinter, followed the lead of Samuel Beckett in incorporating existentialist philosophy, relativism, and the Theater of the Absurd into his plays. Like Pinter, Stoppard is internationally recognized as one in Britain's long line of distinguished dramatists who have been thinkers, and who continue the theater of ideas introduced by Shaw at the end of the nineteenth century.

Stoppard is a dazzler who fires off bursts of sparkling comedic wordplay, and who blends complicated plots with intellectual themes, so that he seems to have moved the theater in the direction of exhilarating cerebral aerobics. His first full-length play, *Rosencrantz and Guildenstern Are Dead* (1966), in which two minor characters in Shakespeare's *Hamlet* witness the unfolding tragedy and then are swept up in it, brought Stoppard instant recognition as a significant playwright in the Beckettian tradition.

Tom Stoppard was born Tomás Sträussler in Zin, Czechoslovakia (now the Czech Republic), the second son and last child of Eugen and Martha Becková Sträussler. Eugen, a company physician for the Bata shoe manufacturing company, was an assimilated Jew. Martha had both gentile and Jewish grandparents. These facts were critical as Germany was preparing war on Europe, and Hitler's virulent anti-Semitism was well known. But Stoppard did not learn he was Jewish until years later. In 1939, as the German invasion of Czechoslovakia was imminent, the family, helped by the benevolent company, fled to the British colony of Singapore. When the Japanese attacked Singapore in 1942, the British evacuated Mrs. Straüssler and the boys to Darjeeling, India. Eugen fatally chose to remain behind until the last possible minute as he was needed in the hospital. When he finally left, his unarmed ship was sunk by the Japanese, and presumably he drowned.

In November 1945, in Calcutta, Martha married Major Kenneth Stoppard of the British Army, attached to the Indian Army. Kenneth was a conservative Briton who was proud to have made his Jewish stepsons British. The family arrived in England and eventually settled in Bristol in 1946. As schoolboys in England, Tomás became Tommy Stoppard and his brother Petr became Peter. In fact, they had replaced the Czech language with English even before they left India.

Stoppard was educated at the Dolphin School, Nottinghamshire, from 1946 to 1948, then attended Pocklington School, Yorkshire, from 1948 to 1954. He then went to work as a journalist with the *Western Daily Press* in Bristol. Four years later he joined the *Bristol Evening World*. While working at the *Evening World*, Stoppard became interested in the theater, and he moved to London to review drama for *Scene*, a short-lived magazine.

After publishing three short stories and writing two radio plays and a television script, Stoppard received a 1964 Ford Foundation grant to attend a colloquium in Berlin for promising young playwrights. For the occasion he wrote a short Shakespearean send-up called *Rosencrantz and Guildenstern Meet King Lear*. That became *Rosencrantz and Guildenstern Are Dead*, produced at the Edinburgh Festival in 1966 and the National Theatre at the Old Vic in 1967. Stoppard's playwriting career was under way. His rise to prominence in the theater was meteoric.

In 1978 Stoppard was made Commander, Order of the British Empire. He was knighted in 1997 and elevated to the Order of Merit by Queen Elizabeth II in 2000.

Of Stoppard's many successful screen and television plays the most famous is the movie *Shakespeare in Love*.

Stoppard married Jose Ingle in 1965. They had two sons. The marriage was dissolved in 1971. He married Miriam Moore-Robinson (born Miriam Stern) in 1972. The couple had two children. They were divorced in 1992. Stoppard had a long-term relationship with the actress Felicity Kendall until 1998.

Jumpers (1968) has a team of acrobats on stage "illustrating" the tortuous discourses of George Moore, a real-life moral philosopher preparing for a competition with Duncan McFee, a logical positivist, for a chair of logic. Meanwhile, his wife, Dotty, has an affair with Sir Archbold Jumpers, the head of the philosophy department who also manages the "Jumpers," philosophical gymnasts. A comical murder investigation of the professor of logic who was shot to death in the beginning adds to the madcap fun.

In *Travesties* (1974), Stoppard intricately theorizes about the relationship between politics and art. Lenin, James Joyce, and the Dadaist artist Tristan Tzara are living in Zürich at the same time. A British official, Henry Carr, does not see the significance of this juxtaposition. Revolutionary politics and revolutionary art are both an acquired taste, and the revolutionary politician and the revolutionary artist share an ambition: changing the course of the world.

Every Good Boy Deserves Favour (1977) deals with injustice as seen through a child's eyes. The child, Sacha, also notes the integrity and courage of his dissenting father. *Night and Day* (1978) concerns journalistic freedom as a way of creating positive political change.

The Real Thing (1982), more naturalistic than most of his

plays, is Stoppard's brilliant, innovative adventure in writing a traditional marital and sexual farce. *Hapgood* (1988) is the name of a British female spy who works with the German–born Kerner, trying to find out if secrets have leaked to the Soviets. Agents may be double or triple. Stoppard asks, What is illusion and what is reality in the world of spies. Kerner knows his science and he applies it to spying. Particles in light–like spies– can become waves that may pass simultaneously through two holes. *Arcadia* (1993), like *Hapgood*, employs contemporary science, combining chaos theory, the laws of thermodynamics, and English landscape gardening at the moment when the history of ideas was shifting from neoclassicism to romanticism: the early nineteenth century.

India Ink (1995) is partly a detective story and partly a love story. The comedy hinges on the farcical misinterpretation of the past by academics as Stoppard focuses on the aesthetic drawbacks of imperial influence. *The Invention of Love* (1997) is about the repressed gay poet A. E. Housman, who in his old age remembers his youthful, unconsummated love for an athletic classmate at Oxford.

The Coast of Utopia (2001) is a trilogy of plays requiring nine hours for performance. In them Stoppard brilliantly explores the satisfactions, excitement, and the pitfalls of the life of the mind. The trilogy focuses on a group of mid–nineteenth-century Russian intellectuals for whom the term "intelligentsia" was coined. The goal of *The Coast of Utopia* is to identify an alternative to communism that would have succeeded through humanistic gradualism where communism so catastrophically failed. The first play, *Voyage*, is set in 1833 on a country estate, where a young radical, Mikhail Bakunin, falls prey to the seduction of revolution. In *Shipwreck*, Bakunin sees that his dreams and his efforts are not without evil results. In *Salvage*, the hero comes to a Tolstoian conclusion: one must focus on the work and not the distant end, which may be a trap, because the world will always be imperfect.

MAJOR PLAYS

Rosencrantz and Guildenstern Are Dead (1966)

In *Rosencrantz and Guildenstern Are Dead*, a play that blends comedy and metaphysical inquiry, Stoppard foregrounds two little people, school friends of Prince Hamlet, who have been summoned by King Claudius and Queen Gertrude to Elsinor to spy on their friend. They are unheroic protagonists who at last have their play although, like the rest of us, they mostly wait in the wings of history. Rosencrantz and Guildenstern and we only catch glimpses of the main-stage tragedy. The young men are almost indistinguishable from each other and have little free will. They are pawns of the mighty, who have almost no feeling or concern for the lowly. Rosencrantz and Guildenstern are very poor spies. They try to manipulate Hamlet, but he easily outfoxes them.

Stoppard has deconstructed *Hamlet*. He has given us a vastly different reading of Shakespeare's play, one that says that chance, not fate, is the determinant in the human experience. Rosencrantz and Guildenstern are executed off stage in Stoppard's play as in Shakespeare's, but at the end of Stoppard's play our sympathies are with our peers, Rosencrantz and Guildenstern, and not with the royals and their courtiers.

The Real Thing (1982)

The Real Thing is a domestic farce within a domestic farce. It begins with Stoppard ambushing the audience, which does not realize until the second scene that the first scene is really an onstage performance of a scene from a play by a character in Stoppard's play, whose name is Henry. The leading male character in Henry's play is an architect named Henry. Charlotte, his wife, has been unfaithful, and Henry's life collapses. The playwright Henry's wife, whose name is also Charlotte, plays Charlotte. The actor who plays Henry the architect is Max, a friend of Henry the playwright and Charlotte the actress.

The next scene is "real life." Clearly Henry and Max's wife, Anne, are having an affair. The couples divorce and Henry and Anne marry. She quickly grows tired of Henry and becomes involved with another playwright, who is not the professional equal of her new husband. The play is ultimately about the reeducation of Henry in relation to the professional, social, emotional, and sexual needs of a wife.

Arcadia (1993)

Arcadia, like Frayn's *Copenhagen*, is not only about science, it is about the indeterminacy that transcends observation and reasoning. To envision life in terms of scientific principles in the relativistic, post–Einsteinian age, Stoppard switches the action of the play between two time periods while maintaining the same setting. The locale is an English country house in 1809 and now. Inanimate objects in the house seem to be able to float between centuries–or perhaps time bends around them? Stoppard, holding the remote so to speak, clicks back and forth between the two eras while employing two sets of characters mirroring each other: for example, Septimus, the family tutor in 1809, and Bernard, a university professor now. Both men write reviews that anger authors–the bad poet, Chater, and the contemporary historian, Hannah, who is also the lady of the house. Both teacher-figures are loved by the daughters of the mansion: Thomasina then, Chloe now. Two characters love mathematics: Thomasina and Gus, a precocious boy.

But passion enters both worlds somewhat incongruously. Gus loves Hannah. Thomasina, who is approaching her seventeenth birthday, loves Septimus. Both younger lovers are rejected. Thomasina dies when a lighted candle she has taken to her bed causes a fire. If Septimus had slept with her, would she have experienced the consummation of hot love instead of the flaming sacrifice she stumbled into? The fire also consumes Septimus's valuable mathematical calculations and the truth about Lord Byron's connection to a death that occurred in the house during his visit in the early years of the nineteenth century. A final waltz attempts to mitigate the feeling that life is mostly about losses and that life's terrifying randomness–its chaos–is unbearable to contemplate. Thomasina is dancing; shortly she will be ashes.

The Invention of Love (1997)

The protagonist of *The Invention of Love* is A. E. Housman, the poet and Latin scholar most famous for having penned *A Shropshire Lad*, an 1896 collection of poems. *The Invention of Love* is a memory play. The poet is dreaming that he has died and is being ferried across the River Styx to Hades (he was a classicist, after all). He is seventy-seven years old as he reflects on his long life. Mostly, he remembers the unrequited love he had for Moses Jackson, a classmate at Oxford, who was a handsome but heterosexual young track star. In flashbacks Housman is his younger self, played by another actor. Saddened in love, Housman turned his passion into poetry. He is contrasted with the ebullient Oscar Wilde, who lived according to his own ethos of self-fulfillment and who rebuked Housman for his passive sullenness when life has so much pleasure to offer.

Stoppard's title is ironic. Love is not real but an invention, perhaps in Housman's case a literary one.

Additional Reading

Billington, Michael. *Stoppard the Playwright*. London: Methuen, 1987.

Flemming, John. *Stoppard's Theatre: Finding Order amid Chaos.* Austin: University of Texas Press, 2002.

Jenkins, Anthony. *The Theatre of Tom Stoppard.* Cambridge: Cambridge University Press, 1989.

Kelly, Katherine E., ed. *The Cambridge Companion to Tom Stoppard.* Cambridge: Cambridge University Press, 2001.

Nadel, Ira. *Tom Stoppard: A Life.* New York: Palgrave Macmillan, 2002.

Rusinko, Susan. *Tom Stoppard.* Boston: Twayne, 1986.

Stoppard, Tom. *Plays: One and Two.* London: Faber and Faber, 1996.

———. *Plays: Three.* London: Faber and Faber, 1998.

———. *Plays: Four.* London: Faber and Faber, 1999.

———. *Plays: Five.* London: Faber and Faber, 1999.

12

The New Sensibilities

Caryl Churchill (1938–)

Caryl Churchill's plays are an especially good example of the new sensibilities in contemporary British drama. Her plays are mainstream, but they espouse such causes as feminism, gay rights, and tolerance and respect for people of color in Britain and elsewhere. Churchill's feminism is particularly British because she incorporates her socialism in it. It is not about the bourgeois-style success of a few women in the "man's world." Those women too often pride themselves on being as good as men in their areas of enterprise. They do little for other women. Churchill would say yes they are women, but they are not sisters. Her agenda calls for collective justice for all women.

Churchill's plays often indict society for allowing the use of violence on women's bodies to control them. Churchill is also well aware of the failure of Western society to recognize and use fully the different perspective women contribute to political life.

Churchill's comedy is parodistic; it is expressed in witty dialogue, mischievous characterizations, and playful dramaturgy. She is acutely aware of speech rhythms. Her main themes are the plight of the powerless, the exploitation of women, and the obsessive dreams that burden human beings.

Churchill is the best-known British woman dramatist. Her

plays are performed all over the world. Churchill was born in London. Her father was a political cartoonist, and her mother was a fashion model, minor film actress, and sometime secretary who had left school at the age of fourteen. The Churchill family emigrated to Canada in 1948, where Churchill was educated at the Trafalgar School in Montreal from 1948 to 1955. Returning to Britain in 1957, Churchill entered Lady Margaret Hall, one of Oxford's colleges for women. While at Oxford, Churchill's early plays were produced by local and university companies. She received a bachelor of arts degree in English in 1960. The next year she married David Harter, a lawyer. The couple has three sons.

During the remainder of the 1960s, Churchill was busy caring for her family. She did, however, write radio and television plays. These plays portrayed the homebound woman's depression. In 1974 Churchill became the first female writer-in-residence at the Royal Court Theatre. Churchill now has written more than fifteen performed stage plays.

In *Owners* (1972), Churchill's first professionally produced play, a group of people become involved in a series of hapless relationships. The play is about motherhood, social control, ownership, and money in a macabre plot in which a mother offers her baby in exchange for a place to live. *Light Shining in Buckinghamshire* (1976) discusses the libertarian ideas and values that led to utopianism in seventeenth-century England, a time period when impoverished women were publicly stripped to the waist and flogged for being contrary, or just unforgivably poor, while middle-class women were terrorized and conditioned to feel self-hatred. Even in church a woman is beaten for trying to speak. It is on the woman's body that church and state inscribe their power.

Vinegar Tom (1976) is about witch hunts in the seventeenth century when the profession of medicine, full of misogyny and run by men, clashed with midwifery and persecuted the women who had been delivering babies safely for generations. When women cannot be controlled and "kept in their place," they are subject to imprisonment, torture, and hanging as witches. Religious and temporal authority combine to persecute the most vulnerable members of society: poor, old, or unmarried women.

Cloud Nine (1979) contrasts the sexual hypocrisy of British colonialism in the Victorian age with the sexual freedom in contemporary Britain. *Top Girls* (1982) features an unmarried woman executive who sacrifices the future of her daughter for her career and lives to regret it. *Fen* (1983) is about the hard life of English women agricultural workers. *Softcops* (1984), a response to Michel Foucault's *Discipline and Punishment*, is an all-male play set in nineteenth-century France that discusses the developing theories and institutions of discipline and punishment as well as the interrelationship of criminals and cops as they subvert authority.

Written like a Restoration play, *Serious Money* (1986), an international hit, is about the City of London, Britain's Wall Street, in the greedy 1980s. The stock market is, of course, the epitome of capitalism and the most worthy of targets for Churchill's socialism. Stock prices are illegally manipulated, a brokerage collapses, third world dictators misappropriate money directed toward their people, and the profit motive rules supreme. Morality is only a public relations ploy. Even murder can be turned into a verdict of suicide if enough money is involved. For Churchill, a life of only making money is no life.

A Mouthful of Birds (1987) presents a picture of women in the thrall of pleasure and violence, often related and mutually satisfying. *Mad Forest: A Play for Romania* (1990) is one of the first dramas on the demise of communism in 1989. It tells the people's story of the fall of the brutal despot Ceausescu. *The Skriker* (1994) is a visionary exploration of urban life, as a kind of female goblin, able to change form at will, stalks two young women to London. The play incorporates music to create an aura of fantastical primitivism. In *Far Away* (2000), a Pinter–like drama, Britain is sinking into authoritarian barbarism. The future is apocalyptic and the end is not far away. *A Number* (2002) is set in the future and concerns the cloning of a boy killed in a car crash at the age of four. After the parents clone multiple copies of the boy, it appears the prototype may not really be dead. Two sons hate the father and one fears that the other, a rival, will kill him.

MAJOR   PLAYS

Cloud Nine (1979)

Cloud Nine is a hilariously outrageous farce that links British imperialism with racism and sexual oppression. Churchill juxtaposes Victorian times with the modern era. She sets the first act in a British colony in Africa during the reign of Queen Victoria and the second act in 1979 London. The same characters are in both scenes even though one hundred years have elapsed between acts.

The cross–casting/cross–dressing is antic. Clive, the colonial administrator and patriarch, is played by a man. His browbeaten wife, Betty, however, is also played by a man, implying the feminist argument that realistic women are not often portrayed on the stage. Edward, the gay son, is played by a woman. He/she is continually exhorted to be more "manly" by his father. Joshua, the native black servant, is played by a white man. Joshua hates his fellow blacks and wants to be treated like a white. The fact that he is played by a white man (like a minstrel in black face) indicates that he is a casualty of colonialism and has been infused with the prevalent imperial racism. Thus he is essentially white. Victoria, the daughter, is played by a rag–doll dummy, indicating that female children in Queen Victoria's time have no voice and no power and therefore can never become adults.

With class and racial discrimination, adultery, bisexual relations, biracial sexual relations, homosexual relations, and pedophilia, everyone in the supposedly straitlaced period is either hypocritical or desperately trying to escape from the restrictions of their designated role and place in society.

In the second act, the cross–sexual casting changes as Churchill offers a less savage view of the modern era. Only Cathy, the daughter of dummy Victoria, is played by a man. That is some progress, but her sexual identity, metaphorically speaking, is still in transit. All in all, however, the sexual climate is more liberal and relaxed, but both the older and younger generations–the Victorian survivors and heirs–are struggling for self-understanding, self-confidence, and self-fulfillment.

Top Girls (1982)

Top Girls, an all–woman play, begins by brilliantly celebrating the achievement of significant women in history or legend. In the long first scene, all the women are top girls in one way or another. The memorable scene is self-contained. Only Marlene, who is hosting the restaurant party to celebrate her promotion to managing director of the Top Girls Employment Agency, connects to the rest of the play, which is realistic. But the very idea of unique, individual achievement is purposely deconstructed by Churchill. Individual achievement, fame, or notoriety of women is of little significance if the societies they lived in were so restricted by patriarchy that only a few exceptional women could break through gender barriers. Often even they found themselves punished for daring to be outstanding.

The subsequent scenes are set in Marlene's employment office and at the East Anglia home of her slatternly, working-class older sister, Joyce, whose "daughter," the psychologically underdeveloped and perhaps slightly retarded Angie turns out to be Marlene's illegitimate child. Joyce has not had the opportunities that Marlene has had, and she is bitter. She realizes that Marlene despises her own impoverished origins and has done everything possible to conceal them. It seems clear that Angie will not have any success in life, but will wind up like the woman she thinks is her mother: locked into a bleak, working-class life. The implied sociological message of the play is that opportunities for women must transcend the class barriers that exist in contemporary Britain.

At the end of the play, Angie wakes up from a bad dream, and mistakes "Aunt" Marlene for her "mother." She would like to live with Marlene and grow up like Marlene, but her future will be Joyce's not Marlene's, no matter what the latter will do for her. Marlene sacrificed Angie in order to have her career. Her guilt is palpable. No woman should have to make that decision.

Additional Reading

Churchill, Caryl. *Plays*. London: Methuen, 1985.

Kritzer, Amelia Howe. *The Plays of Caryl Churchill: Theatre of Empowerment*. New York: St. Martin's, 1991.

Randall, Phyllis R., ed. *Caryl Churchill: A Casebook*. New York: Garland, 1989.

Shelagh Delaney (1939–)

In 1957 a young woman from Salford, Lancashire, saw a touring performance of Terence Rattigan's unsuccessful *Variations on a Theme*. She was so outraged by what she saw as a ridiculous, cringing attitude toward homosexuality that she sat

down and wrote a play that did not disguise or merely imply
a character's homosexuality but came right out with it. The
nineteen–year–old was Shelagh Delaney, and the play, a smash
hit for its unvarnished realism when directed by Joan Littlewood for the Theatre Workshop in 1958, was *A Taste of Honey*.
Simply put, the play is about a girl left to spend Christmas
alone by her forty–year–old mother who has gone off to celebrate the holiday with her latest boyfriend. The daughter
sleeps with a black sailor who leaves her pregnant, and a gentle, gay art student moves in and takes care of her until the
baby is almost due. Jo and Geof are a family until Jo's mother
returns and breaks it up. The play is a very early depiction of
homosexuality on the British stage, and it took kitchen sink
drama into a new area.

After *A Taste of Honey*, Delaney wrote two more plays: *The
Lion in Love* (1960), a study of a hopeless marriage, and *The House
That Jack Built* (1979). Both failed and Delaney early on turned to
writing for television and film.

Delaney was born in Salford, an industrial suburb of Manchester. Her father was a transport worker and her mother was
a homemaker. She was educated at Broughton secondary
school after which she worked at various jobs including sales-
girl, clerk, and usher in a movie house. It was of course *A Taste
of Honey* that started Delaney on her writing career. Much of her
life has been spent in London and with her mother in Salford.
Delaney rewrote *A Taste of Honey* into an award–winning film.
Delaney is a single mother with a daughter.

M A J O R   P L A Y

A Taste of Honey (1958)
A Taste of Honey is a sentimental, bittersweet drama, but it
does touch on some serious questions such as the role of homosexuality in a relationship that is marriage–like, the ques-

tion of abortion, what life is like for working-class girls, and the status of a so-called illegitimate child.

At the open Helen, a tart, and her teenage daughter Josephine are moving into a shabby flat in a Manchester slum. Helen becomes engaged to her latest boyfriend, Peter, who is ten years younger than she is. Peter and Helen leave Jo to fend for herself. Helen has never claimed to be a responsible mother. Alone in the flat and lonely, Jo invites her boyfriend Jimmy, a black sailor, to stay with her over the Christmas holiday.

In act 2 Jimmy has left, and Jo asks Geof, a young, gay, art student to move in with her. He has no place to live because his landlady has thrown him out. Jo is pregnant and is upset. She does not want to be a mother. She is not even ready to be a woman. When Geof learns of Jo's condition, and that Jimmy has returned to the sea as sailors do, he becomes Jo's surrogate mother. But when her real mother returns, she also unceremoniously throws Geof out.

The perspective of the play is a woman's. Jo has learned something very important in her days with Geof: a mother does have responsibility for bringing up a child. Jo has matured somewhat. As a mother-to-be she now feels important. She could almost take care of Helen. The mother-daughter relationship has changed. The taste of honey is the life Jo had with Geof before Helen returned, a life without the complexity of sex, a prelapsarian interlude for a child who is about to become a woman too soon.

Additional Reading
Delaney, Shelagh. *A Taste of Honey: A Play.* London: Methuen, 1959.

Alan Ayckbourn (1939–)

The prolific Alan Ayckbourn is Britain's most popular living writer of comedy for the stage. He has written some fifty-seven plays. Although they are performed around the world, his plays are distinctly British. His subjects are the complications of suburban and middle-class life, sexual dysfunction, social anxiety, and crushed ambition. His characters are typically British: restrained, reserved, and reclusive. They are concerned with class and–secretly–with sex. Ayckbourn's women are sympathetically drawn. He sees their lives in the contemporary world as particularly stressed. Ayckbourn's main audience is the same middle class that peoples his plays. His plots are intricate, well-made farces; still, they are deeper than traditional farces and perhaps are best described as domestic comedies.

Ayckbourn was born in London, the only child of Horace Ayckbourn, first violinist and deputy leader of the London Symphony Orchestra, and the former Irene Maud Worley, a writer. When Alan was five years old, his mother divorced his father and married a bank manager for Barclay's Bank who was not fond of his stepson. The second marriage was doomed, but before the breakup Ayckbourn lived in a succession of small towns with branches of the bank. Ayckbourn was educated at Haileybury School, Hertford, and Imperial Service College in Hertfordshire from 1952 to 1956. He then trained as an actor and stage manager with Donald Wolfit's traveling company, performing all over England and Scotland from 1956 to 1957. Then he became an actor and stage manager for the Stephen Joseph Theatre-in-the-Round in Scarborough, Yorkshire, from 1957 to 1962.

Ayckbourn began his playwriting career in 1959 with *The Square Cat*. After several directing appointments and a stint as drama producer for BBC Radio, Leeds, from 1964 to 1970, Ayckbourn returned to the Stephen Joseph Theatre-in-the-Round in 1970 as permanent artistic director. There he has directed the initial performances of almost all his plays.

In 1987 Ayckbourn was made a Commander, Order of the British Empire. In 1997 he was knighted. Ayckbourn married

Christine Helen Roland in 1959. They had two sons and were divorced in 1997. That same year Ayckbourn married his long-time companion Heather Stoney, an actress.

Relatively Speaking (1967) depicts all the possible ways people can be embarrassed. Indeed, embarrassment is a major emotion in Ayckbourn's comedy. *How the Other Half Loves* (1969) employs two halves of the set to show two living rooms in two homes with contrasting furniture. The households are linked by an adulterous affair. The adulterers use a third couple for excuses, but collisions and confusions abound. In *Absurd Person Singular* (1973) Ayckbourne amazingly makes the attempted suicide of a girl a successful subject for farce.

The three plays of *The Norman Conquests* (1973) constitute Ayckbourn's most ingenious and best-known work. In *Absent Friends* (1974), Ayckbourn gets humor out of the way people laugh at inappropriate times. *Bedroom Farce* (1977) employs a Georges Feydeau farcical situation with lots of lost clothing and eight people in three bedrooms.

Just between Ourselves (1977) portrays a well-meaning husband driving his wife to insanity through his constant cheerfulness and optimism. *Joking Apart* (1978) is a funny yet serious discourse on obsessive love and collapsing marriages. In *Sisterly Feelings* (1979), married sisters fight over an attractive outsider, to the anger of their spouses.

In *A Chorus of Disapproval* (1986), a provincial theater troupe searches for a leading man. Their choice commences bedding every woman in sight. *Women in Mind* (1986) is about the sexual objectification of women by men and the negative effect of marriage on women.

A Small Family Business (1987) depicts a greedy, Mafia-like family at a party that exposes adultery, drug addiction, and an alienated younger generation destined for the ranks of the unemployed. *The Revengers' Comedies* (1991) makes farce out of serial killing and inept dueling with pistols. *Things We Do for Love* (1998) is a clever rewrite of Noël Coward's classic *Private Lives* (1930) but with more explicit sex and violence.

Put the titles of *House* (1999) and *Garden* (1999) together and one comes up with the title of the middle- to upper-middle-class magazine. The magazine is much concerned with appearances and so are the plays. The plays take place on the same day between 8 A.M. and 6 P.M., the day of the village fair. Adultery is rampant, and class and as well as marital barriers come crashing down. *Whenever* (2000) is a musical about time travel. In the trilogy *Damsels in Distress* (2002), all the plays are set in the same upscale London flat where careful planning is thwarted by various nemeses. In *GamePlan*, the daughter of a single mother tries to help out by turning to prostitution and her first client drops dead. In *FlatSpin*, an out-of-work actress pretends to own the flat and gets caught. And in *RolePlay*, a middle-class dinner party is upset by intruding low-lifes.

M A J O R   P L A Y S

The Norman Conquests: Table Manners, Living Together, Round and Round the Garden (1973)

The plays in *The Norman Conquests* can be performed singularly, with the audience experiencing closure at the end of each. Or the trilogy can be put on in successive evenings with the audience looking forward to the next play. The overall title refers to the main character, Norman, a man who thinks himself a great lover because he is somewhat attractive to women. In fact he is unkempt and scruffy, certainly not the typical ladykiller, but the women in the plays do not have the opportunities to do better. Norman is an assistant librarian. His sexual fantasies seem to come from the books he reads. The milieu of the play is the British middle class, with husbands in business and wives organizing charities. But Norman's wife, Ruth, has her own career. She is near-sighted, but because of vanity she will not wear her glasses. If she did she would see what kind of world Norman inhabits.

The plays take place over a weekend. Encounters take place in corners. The first setting, *Table Manners*, is the dining room of a run-down Victorian house in which live unmarried Annie, Ruth's sister, and their bed-ridden mother, and to which Norman and Ruth and Reg, Ruth's brother, and Sarah, Reg's wife, have come. The mother is a demanding person. Annie reads romance novels and has fantasies that are somewhat similar to Norman's. *Living Together* confides what is happening in the sitting room during the weekend. In *Round and Round the Garden*, the story moves out-of-doors and the plots come to closure.

Norman is plotting to take Annie, his sister-in-law, to a hotel on a weekend tryst. Ruth's brother Reg, a real estate agent, and his wife, Sarah, come to take care of the mother because they think Annie is going off for a fling with Tom, a dim-witted, reluctant veterinarian suitor. Annie is not sure if Tom will be administering to her cat or protesting his love, which she is not sure she really wants to hear. Sarah worms the information about the assignation out of Annie and, morally outraged, sets out to wreck the would-be lovers' plan. Then sexual jealousy replaces moral outrage when Norman comes on to Sarah with a similar proposition to the one he had offered Annie. Ruth, now more aware of the desires of her would-be lothario husband, sets out to reclaim Norman.

The situations for women are awful. They are lonely. Those unfortunate enough to be married are bossed by unfeeling and incompetent men. Poor Annie is a slave to her mother. The title of the trilogy purposely trivializes British history. Ayckbourn's Britons are anything but heroic.

Additional Reading

Allen, Paul. *Alan Ayckbourn: Grinning at the Edge: A Biography.* London: Methuen, 2001.

Ayckbourn, Alan. *The Norman Conquest: A Trilogy of Plays.* New York: Nelson Doubleday, 1975.

———. *Three Plays.* New York: Grove, 1975.

Billington, Michael. *Alan Ayckbourn.* New York: Grove, 1984.

Dukore, Bernard Frank. *Alan Ayckbourn: A Casebook.* New York: Garland, 1991.

Kalson, Albert E. *Laughter in the Dark: The Plays of Alan Ayckbourn.* Rutherford, N.J.: Fairleigh Dickinson University Press, 1993.

White, Sydney. *Alan Ayckbourn.* Boston: Twayne, 1989.

Michelene Wandor (1940–)

As well as writing plays, Michelene Wandor has published poetry, fiction, and drama criticism. In the latter arena she is acknowledged as a leading feminist spokesperson on sexual politics and gender issues in modern British drama. Wandor has worked energetically with the Royal National Theatre as well as with fringe venues and feminist collectives. Feminist politics, gender questions, family structure, and social activism continue to inform her work.

Wandor was born in London, the daughter of Abraham Jonah Samuels, a tailor, and Rosalie Wander Samuels. She was educated in Essex at Chingford Secondary Modern School from 1954 to 1956 and Chingford County High School from 1956 to 1959. She then studied at Newnham College, Cambridge, from 1959 to 1962, receiving the bachelor of arts degree in English (with honors) in 1962. While working as an editor and a drama reviewer, Wandor began to write plays herself. Her first production was *You Too Can Be Ticklish* (1971). From 1974 to 1975

Wandor studied at the University of Essex, Colchester, receiving the master of arts degree in sociology in 1975. Currently she is a senior lecturer in creative writing at the University of North London. Wandor married Edward Victor, a literary agent, in 1963. They had two children and were divorced in 1975. Besides writing more than fifteen produced plays, Wandor has written many successful radio and television scripts.

Care and Control (1977) was one of the first political dramas to address the role of the state in regard to motherhood. In *Whores d'Oeuvres* (1978), Wandor discusses the age-old exploitation of women through prostitution. The play also raises the question of whether prostitution is also a means through which a poor person can achieve independence. This is a question Shaw raises in *Mrs Warren's Profession*, written in 1893. *Aid Thy Neighbour* (1978) discusses the issue of artificial insemination in a frank way.

Aurora Leigh (1979) is a successful adaptation of Elizabeth Barrett Browning's verse novel in which the iambic pentameter of the original is retained. Another successful adaptation is *The Wandering Jew* (1987), from Eugène Sue's novel. The play was coauthored with Mike Alfreds. *Wanted* (1988) marks a turn away from social realism in Wandor's drama. It is based on the biblical Sarah, wife of Abraham, who gave birth at age ninety.

Additional Reading
Wandor, Michelene: *Five Plays*. London: Journeyman Press, 1984.

Howard Brenton (1942–)

Howard Brenton, a socialist dramatist, is convinced that all plays are political. Despite the fact that the general theater audience is a bourgeois one, he has been determined to confront it with what he sees as the corruption of British capitalism. For

Brenton the polemicist, Britain has deteriorated into class confrontations, violence, and social anger. Institutions are failing. Politicians and police work hand in hand to keep the people down. The government is contemptible. Brenton's righteous passion and indignation remain an inspiration for the young British playwrights of today.

Brenton's best-known play is *The Romans in Britain* (1980), a parable in which the Roman occupation of Britain is linked to the presence of the British Army in Northern Ireland. Many critics and audience members were angered by the analogy. Others were shocked by a scene in which a Roman soldier attempts a homosexual rape of a young Celt. The scene led to a court case, later abandoned. *The Romans in Britain* is also a history play about events that changed the lives and society of the Celtic people who lived in what is now England during and after the invasion by Julius Caesar in 54 B.C.

There is much violence in Brenton's plays. They are full of pus, blood, and broken flesh. It gets the audience's attention. But of course, these are the ingredients of life and death.

Brenton was born in Portsmouth, Hampshire, the son of a policeman who became a Methodist minister. He was educated at Chichester High School and at St. Catherine's College, Cambridge, where he received the bachelor of arts degree (with honors) in English in 1965. His first play, *Ladders of Fools*, was produced at Cambridge the year of his graduation. Brenton went on to work as a stage manger, an occasional actor, and, from 1972 to 1973, resident dramatist at the Royal Court Theatre. Brenton married Jane Fry in 1970. The couple has two sons.

Revenge (1969) depicts a criminal bent on killing a certain Scotland Yard investigator. Each operates under a separate but comparable code, the mobster's and the Calvinist's. In *Christie in Love* (1969), a powerful, one-act play about an actual murderer, John Reginald Christie, Brenton paints the police as just as violent in enforcing their middle-class morality as the criminal Christie is in his killings. *Magnificence* (1973) depicts young radicals trying peaceful means for social change, but when frustrated they resort to violence and are killed themselves.

The two plays in which Brenton collaborated with David Hare, *Brassneck* (1973) and *Pravda: A Fleet Street Comedy* (1985), contain some of his best work. The former shows the decay of Britain over a thirty-year period, and the latter is a vitriolic attack on the media barons of our time.

The Churchill Play (1974), commissioned by the National Theatre, is set in an Orwellian Britain that looks like the old Soviet Union or Nazi Germany. Winston Churchill comes to life, holding a cigar and carrying a Union Jack. His wartime accomplishments are derided because the working class survived World War II despite him. *Greenland* (1978) is a psychodrama set in the future. *Berlin Bertie* (1992) is about the loss of faith in communism as a former Stasi officer from the defunct German Democratic Republic comes to London and goes into the pornography business. This play breaks with Brenton's penchant for spectacle and Brechtian agitprop.

Additional Reading
Brenton, Howard. *Plays: One*. London: Methuen, 1986.
——. *Plays: Two*. London: Methuen, 1989.
Wilson, Ann. *Howard Brenton: A Casebook*. New York: Garland, 1992.

Christopher Hampton (1946–)

Christopher Hampton has generally avoided the more radical forms of modern British drama such as the Theater of the Absurd, kitchen sink drama, and the theater of cruelty. He has given much effort to adapting the works of other playwrights—such as Isaac Babel, Henrik Ibsen, Anton Chekhov, Moliére, and

Pierre Choderlos de Laclos, the eighteenth-century author of the novel *Les Liaisons Dangereuses*–partially as a result of a life-long interest in foreign languages.

Hampton is a craftsman of the theater. Style is Hampton's forte, wit is his pleasure, and like Shaw, he sees the stage as a platform for debating ideas.

Christopher James Hampton was born in Fayal, the Azores, where his father was working as an engineer. He was first educated at schools in Aden and in Alexandria, places where his father was posted. In 1956 the Hampton family had to flee Egypt when the Suez crisis broke out. His family then left him as a boarder at a preparatory school. Then from 1959 to 1963, he attended Lancing College, Sussex, where he was an outstanding student. From 1964 to 1968 Hampton studied modern languages at New College, Oxford, from which he received the bachelor of arts and master of arts degrees. At Oxford he joined the dramatic society. Early success in the theater allowed Hampton to live the writer's life. He has also written for the musical stage, radio, and television.

Hampton married Laura Margaret de Holesch, a social worker and a nurse, in 1971. The couple has two children.

Hampton's first original play, *When Did You Last See My Mother?* (1966), produced at the Royal Court Theatre when Hampton was still an undergraduate, is about two public school chums, one of whom later has a sexual relationship with his friend's mother. In *Total Eclipse* (1968), Hampton discusses the sexual relationship between two great French poets, Paul Verlaine, who was twenty-six years old, and Arthur Rimbaud, who was sixteen. The play is also about the nature and significance of poetry. *The Philanthropist* (1970) is concerned with art and academia. It is Hampton's best-known play.

Savages (1973) is about the complex truths of genocide. In *Tales of Hollywood* (1982), Hampton finally challenges the powerful grip of Brecht's theatricality. His protagonist, a playwright like himself, avoids the chains of dogmatic conviction. *White Chameleon* (1991) is set in Alexandria, Egypt, from 1952 to 1956. There an English family is affected by the great social upheaval in the country leading up to the Suez War in 1956. *The Talking Cure* (2003) is based on the early history of psychoanalysis and a love triangle consisting of Freud, Jung, and their patient, Sabina Spielrein.

MAJOR PLAY

The Philanthropist (1970)

At the opening of the play, a biting academic comedy of manners, Oxford dons in a comfortable college room are deep in discussion of the appropriateness of the suicidal ending of a drama, which the author goes on to demonstrate with a fake gunshot. When the act ends, however, the author actually commits suicide by shooting himself. The suicide, the torching of a college by a disillusioned student, and the news of the murder of the entire British government cabinet, including the prime minister, do not affect the insulated academic life of the dons. Worldly violence is of little concern to them. Instead they focus on word and sexual games.

The play's protagonist is Philip, a philologist as well as a philanthropist who enjoys word games and also loves humanity. He engages in witty debates on art and language. But the dons are not only interested in irony and clever paradoxes, they also delight in Philip's declining fortunes. They are vain, corrupt, backbiting, and hypocritical. The audience feels as though they have been exposed to the kind of academic secrets they would rather not have been privy to.

The Philanthropist is partially based on Molière's *Misanthrope*.

Additional Reading

Francis, Ben. *Christopher Hampton: Dramatic Ironist.* Oxford: Amber Lane, 1996.

Gross, Robert. *Christopher Hampton: A Casebook.* New York: Garland, 1990.

Hampton, Christopher. *Plays.* London: Faber and Faber, 1997.

Howard Barker (1946–)

One of Brecht's uncompromising British disciples, Howard Barker surprises audiences by setting his plays in unexpected places. Barker is opposed to naturalistic drama. He deplores the degeneration of morality in British political life, and hopes for a reconstruction of society according to socialist values.

Barker's theatrical world is one of continual disorder, where betrayal is the currency of human relations, and catastrophe, like smoke from a burning city, is always in the air. Wars structure Barker's dramas. His plays contain a volatile mixture of sex, vitriol, and passion. His humor is grim. He seems to want to offend his audience, knowing that what offends today does not offend tomorrow.

London-born Barker was educated at Battersea Grammar School from 1958 to 1964 and at Sussex University, Brighton, from 1964 to 1968. He received the master of arts degree in history from Sussex in 1968. He has been resident dramatist for the Open Space Theatre in London, and the Wrestling School Theater Company in London. The latter was founded in 1988 just to perform Barker's plays. Barker has written for radio, television, and films. Four collections of his poetry have been published. Barker married Sandra Law in 1972. They have one child.

Barker's first play, *Stripwell* (1975), portrays moral collapse and class revenge. *Claw* (1975) depicts a kind of rake's progress.

A working-class lad betrays his class, gets involved with political scandal, and is killed by the police. *Fair Slaughter* (1977) is a sequel to *Claw*. It demands that people criticize any and all ideologies. *That Good between Us* (1977) has a female Labour Party home secretary given unlimited power over society. Inevitably, she is complicit in a serious of damning compromises. Death is her reward for betrayal of the people.

The Hang of the Gaol (1978) shows a dying Britain as a vast prison for its people because of the impotence of social democracy. *The Love of a Good Man* (1978) is a dark and savage comedy about World War I profiteering. *The Loud Boy's Life* (1980) shows the rise to power of a right-wing demagogue. *No End of Blame: Scenes of Overcoming* (1981) is a highly regarded drama whose hero is an artist. In the army in World War I, he sees that national service leads to carnage. Communism is the initial answer to social injustice, but eventually he sees that the important thing is resisting the worship of any ideology.

The ironically titled *Victory* (1983) is set in the Restoration. A widow carries around the exhumed remains of her husband, once a member of the parliamentary forces under Cromwell that executed Charles I. Half-mad, she treasures the remains as a reminder of a time when England hoped for a better government. *The Power of the Dogg* (1984) has Europe divided between Stalin and Churchill at the Yalta Conference in 1945.

The Castle (1985), *Scenes from an Execution* (1985), and *Downchild* (1985) are history plays. *Pity in History* (1986) is another play about the seventeenth-century English civil war. *Seven Lears* (1989) is Barker's irreverent parody of Shakespeare's tragedy. He portrays Lear shuttling between his wife and his mistress as he causes mayhem in Britain. *The Europeans* (1990) is set just after the siege of Vienna by the Turks is lifted in 1684. The Austrian hero's lover has been raped and mutilated by the Turks, and she insists that all in the city see what happens to a woman in war. *A Hard Heart* (1992) is set in ancient Greece where the queen appeals to an architect to help save her city. They fail because of the treachery of her son. *A Birth*, a scene excerpted from Barker's prose epic, *The Ecstatic Bible*, was performed in 2000. Barker attempts to redeem Hamlet's mother in *Gertrude–The Cry* (2002), but his queen is a predator.

Additional Reading

Barker, Howard. *Arguments for the Theatre*. Manchester: Manchester University Press, 1998.

——. *Collected Plays*. London: Riverrun, 1990.

Rabe, David Ian. *Howard Barker: Politics and Desire: An Expository Study of His Drama and His Poetry, 1969–1987*. New York: St. Martin's, 1989.

David Hare (1947–)

David Hare creates vivid spaces for the settings of his plays. They may be country houses or boarding houses, artists' digs or tacky nightclubs. All have a blend of reality and mystery that evokes memories of Graham Greene novels. There is a resonance of something or someone missing or lost. It may be a person or it may be a virtue. Hare asks the moral question: how does being a good and decent human being change other people's lives for the better? This is Graham Greene's great question too.

Hare was born in the coastal town of St. Leonards, Sussex. His father was a ship's purser. Hare spent much of his childhood with his sister in nearby Bexhill-on-the-Sea. He was educated at Lancing College, Sussex. Among his classmates were the playwright Christopher Hampton and the lyricist Tim Rice. From 1964 to 1968, Hare studied English at Jesus College, Cambridge, where he met and became friends with Germaine Greer, the feminist writer, who was a graduate student in English. Hare received the master of arts degree in English in 1968.

After Cambridge, Hare and Tony Bicat founded a touring company called the Portable Theatre. Hare only remained affiliated with the company three years, but he wrote two plays during that time and determined to be a professional dramatist. In 1969 Hare became literary manager and then resident playwright at the Royal Court although he was writing for other theater groups. After 1971 Hare had various appointments as a resident dramatist and opportunities to direct plays by others. He worked with the Joint Stock Company, which he cofounded, from 1973 to 1980. Since 1984 he has been an associate director of the National Theatre. David Hare was knighted in 1998.

Hare has had significant success writing plays for television and film. Hare married Margaret Matheson in 1970. They had three children and divorced in 1980.

Hare's first important play is *What Happened to Blake?* (1970) in which Hare attempts to reproduce the thought processes of the early Romantic poet and artist William Blake. *Slag* (1970) is a play Hare latter repudiated as shameful. It is set in a girls' public school, where three teachers will forgo sex with men in order to help establish a just socialist society. It is a mean and uninformed attack on feminism. *The Great Exhibition* (1972) paints a portrait of a foolish, defeated Labour Party member of Parliament while exposing the underbelly of contemporary politics.

Teeth 'n' Smiles (1972) uses the Titanic as a symbol of sinking Britain. In the thriller *Knuckle* (1974), a sleazy British arms dealer is searching for his missing sister in a dark world of betrayal and murder. To his surprise, she turns out to be a political radical. *Fanshen* (1975), based on a book by William Hinton, is set in a Chinese village in the immediate aftermath of World War II when China was being turned into a communist state. (The title is Mandarin for "turn over.") In a series of powerful Brechtian tableaux, the audience is asked to examine the way Chinese society is being reorganized.

Hare and Howard Brenton had two outstanding collaborations: *Brassneck* (1973), about Britain's decay in a thirty-year period, and a satire on media moguls, *Pravda: A Fleet Street Comedy* (1985).

The international hit *Plenty* (1978) is the story of post–World War II disillusion. In the well-received *A Map of the World* (1983), a novel written by a character in the play, based on an incident in his life, is being filmed as participants in a UNESCO world hunger conference in a third world country debate their antagonistic positions. Hare cinematically intercuts camera scenes with reenacted recollections. At the hunger conference, an Indian author and a liberal British journalist engage in a Shavian ideological debate after competing for the favors of a young American woman.

The Secret Rapture (1989) depicts a self-righteous, ultraconservative, female British government minister converted to socialism by the murder of her selfless socialist sister. The title refers to spiritual love and Christian martyrdom. In *Racing Demon* (1990), English priests struggle to do good despite the fact that their church, the Church of England, is corrupt. *Murmuring Judges* (1991) attacks British courts and the justice system.

The Absence of War (1993) is a trilogy about the British Labour Party and the fundamental institutions of British society, which Hare perceived as morally bankrupt. The plays were designed, in the manner of Shaw, to set off a national debate.

Skylight (1995) uses the restaurant business to symbolize consumer society and the unproductive ways it uses money. *Amy's View* (1997) contains fine characterizations. It is a story of mothers and daughters, and reminds audiences that one never knows how things will turn out with children. It is also a bit of a theater parody.

The *Judas Kiss* (1998) embraces a notorious story: Oscar Wilde's fatal attraction for the beautiful but neurotic Lord Alfred Douglas. *Via Dolorosa* (1998) is a one-man show about the Palestine problem. Hare has performed it. *The Blue Room* (1998) is a sexually charged, successful version of Arthur Schnitzler's *Reigen* (better known as *La Ronde*). *The Breath of Life* (2002) has two middle-aged women, a man's wife and his mistress, meet for the first time. The man has fled them both for another woman. The encounter is sad and humorous. *Permanent Way* (2003) discusses the cost of the privatization of the British Railways. *Stuff Happens* (2004) is a documentary drama about the war in Iraq.

MAJOR PLAY

Plenty (1978)

Plenty tells the story of a brave Englishwoman, Susan Traherne, who is parachuted into German-occupied France during World War II. Her spy mission is exceedingly dangerous, but she survives. She is not only a woman of valor, she is a woman with great integrity. Postwar Britain is not comfortable with such integrity. Her life begins to spiral down through drinking, embarrassing behavior, and hurting her husband, until a breakdown occurs. The audience wonders what more can happen to her. A miserable death? Instead, in a brilliant piece of dramatic writing, Hare shows the old and bitter woman going back in time through good days and bad. She becomes young and beautiful once more. It is France and the sun is shining. Her exciting life is just beginning. The play ends with her feeling hope once more. It is a false hope of course, but the irony is only partly felt by the audience, for they have seen what they wish for themselves.

Additional Reading

Donesky, Finley. *David Hare: Moral and Historical Perspectives*. Westport, Conn.: Greenwood, 1996.

Fitzpatrick, John. *David Hare*. Boston: Twayne, 1990.

Hare, David. *Plays: One*. London: Faber and Faber, 1996.

——. *Plays: Two*. London: Faber and Faber, 1997.

Homden, Carol. *The Plays of David Hare*. Cambridge: Cambridge University Press, 1995.

Zeifman, Hersh. *David Hare: A Casebook*. New York: Garland, 1994.

Willy Russell (1947–)

In his plays Willy Russell has highlighted the barriers between the rich and the poor, and between the highly educated and the less educated. His vision is socialist; his agenda is to promote the liberation of working-class people in general, and women in particular, from the mindless escapism of popular culture, that is, commercial pop songs and the worship of media idols. Russell clearly believes that there is much goodness in human beings. He has striven to show that in his gentle dramas.

William Martin Russell was born in Whiston, Lancashire. His early education was at schools in Knowsley and Rainford, Lancashire. He attended the Childwald College of Further Education, Liverpool, from 1969 to 1970. He entered St. Katharine's College of Higher Education in 1970, receiving the certificate of education in 1973.

While studying, Russell worked as a women's hairdresser in Liverpool and Kirby from 1963 to 1968. From that time to becoming a full-time writer, Russell was employed as a laborer and a comprehensive school teacher.

Russell has also written for radio, television, and the screen. In the latter regard, he wrote the successful screenplays for his two most famous plays: *Educating Rita* and *Shirley Valentine*. Russell married Ann Margaret Seagroatt in 1969. They have three children.

Drawing on his Liverpool background, Russell wrote the

musical *John, Paul, George, Ringo . . . and Bert* (1974). *Breezeblock Park* (1975) tells the story of two sisters, Betty and Reeny, who try to outdo each other in conspicuous consumption. Their territory is the home, while their men live for sports and politics. When Betty's daughter becomes pregnant, the sisters join forces and their competition ends. *Stags and Hens* (1978) is about the imminent failure of a wedding with a drunk for the groom. The bride escapes marital disaster.

When employed as a hairdresser, Russell came to know how women talk about the hopes, goals, and disappointments in their lives. The broadly humorous satire *Educating Rita* (1980) is a moving play about the importance of aspirations, especially for working-class people who have much more to overcome than do their bourgeois fellow citizens. It is also a somewhat abrasive commentary on the privileged life of academics. Rita takes an Open University extension course. She wants to shed her working-class background though haute culture and general knowledge. Her tutor, Frank, can help her access it. By the end of the play, she gains sophistication. She knows what to wear and what to see in the theater. But she also has contempt for Frank because of his weaknesses and inability to appreciate how easy his life has been.

Blood Brothers (1983) is a musical about two brothers who were separated at birth and reared in different social classes: one is working class and the other is middle class. Russell shows how much more significant environment is than genetic inheritance. Each brother sees the other as having the better life. In the melodramatic ending, one brother kills the other and the police shoot the survivor.

Shirley Valentine (1986) is a brilliant two-act monologue by Shirley in "woman speak." Shirley is a forty-two-year-old Liverpool housewife. The play begins in her kitchen and moves to a low-class *taverna* in Greece to which she has escaped with the help of a feminist friend. Shirley has left behind her boorish mate and their two selfish and lazy children. In warm and beautiful Greece she has an affair with a waiter, who she well knows seduces English women regularly. No matter–his courting and compliments have rebuilt her self-esteem. The depressed woman's fantasy ends with Shirley waiting on tables and expecting her husband to arrive and try to get her back. Shirley is an older Rita who did not try for education and class change when younger.

Additional Reading
Russell, Willy. *Plays*. London: Methuen, 1996.

David Edgar (1948–)

David Edgar is a prolific playwright. More than fifty of his plays have been produced. He is a socialist polemicist, but perhaps more like Shaw than Brecht in that–especially most recently–he uses argument more than image to inform. Edgar wants us to examine change as well as understand our times and ourselves by showing us how the process of history affects us.

Edgar's plays tend to be somewhat abstract. The private experience is less important than the theme and political purpose. Characters are motivated more by their class than by their individual psychology. Subjective perceptions are not reality. Edgar strives to affect conscience not only in a character but in the audience, which must be made to understand the cost and the complications of political actions.

Edgar received prominent recognition in 1976 when his epic drama *Destiny*, a study of the roots of fascism and racism in British society in the post–World War II period, was produced by the Royal Shakespeare Company. The second landmark in Edgar's career was his vastly successful 1980 adaptation of

Dickens's *The Life and Adventures of Nicholas Nickelby,* also produced by the RSC in London and on Broadway. The third landmark of Edgar's progressing career was *Maydays,* a chronicle of the post–World War II Left, in which Edgar depicts the significant May Day holidays of socialism in the period. *Maydays* was the first contemporary play produced by the RSC in the Barbican Theatre. Obviously, Edgar never fears to engage complex themes and historical events with compendiousness.

Edgar was born in Birmingham. His father was a television producer and his mother was an actress. He was educated at Oundle School, Northamptonshire, from 1961 to 1965, and then from 1966 to 1969 at the University of Manchester, from which he received the bachelor of arts degree in drama. At Manchester Edgar also became involved in campus politics, but even as a child he had followed his father's interest in the British political scene. After university Edgar went to work as a journalist for the *Bradford Telegraph and Argus* in Yorkshire from 1969 to 1972. From then on, Edgar devoted himself to playwriting, beginning with a long association with the General Will radical theater company. Edgar has also written for radio and television. Edgar's wife Eva, a former Labour Party city counselor in Birmingham, died of cancer in 1998.

Tedderella (1971) is about Prime Minister Edward Heath and the British attempt to enter the Common Market. *Dick Deterred* (1973) is a melodrama based on the career of Richard Nixon and the Watergate scandal.

Wreckers (1977), set in London's East End, shows how the working class can act in solidarity against injustice but still maintain respect and space for individualism. *The Jail Diary of Albie Sachs* (1978) attacks apartheid by presenting the ordeal of an imprisoned white South African lawyer. *Mary Barnes* (1978) projects the new thinking on schizophrenia as contrasted with the brutal treatment of these ill people in earlier times. Commissioned by the feminist theater company Monstrous Regiment, the successful *Teendreams* (1979) depicts the emerging awareness of specifically feminist needs and the concomitant agenda in post-1968 Britain.

Entertaining Strangers: A Play for Dorchester (1985) has the people of the city of Dorchester examine their own history. *That Summer* (1987) treats the tragic British coal miners' strike of 1985. *The Shape of the Table* (1990) discusses the struggles of Eastern European countries to establish new governments after the fall of communism. *Pentecost* (1994) treats the chaos that the end of Soviet hegemony caused in the Balkans. *Albert Speer* (1999), a biographical play about the life of Hitler's favorite architect, who planned the future Berlin and was Nazi Germany's minister of armament, is a powerful and disturbing play about the fascination of evil, temptations of power, and denial of guilt.

In 2003 Edgar presented an intellectual two-play cycle drama, *Continental Divide*, about American politics for American audiences. *Mothers Against* depicts a political candidate whose daughter is an eco-terrorist. *Daughters of the Revolution* has political radicals of the 1960s coming together again to support their liberal candidate. Like Shakespeare's history plays in which the Lancasters battle the Yorkists, *Continental Divide* has two warring camps, the Democrats and the Republicans, and the political prize is the super state: California. Edgar's slant on American politics is decidedly left.

Additional Reading

Edgar, David. *Albert Speer*. London: Nick Hern, 2000.

———. *Plays: Two*. London: Methuen, 1990.

———. *Plays: Three*. London: Methuen, 1991.

Swain, Elizabeth. *David Edgar: Playwright and Politician*. New York: P. Lang, 1986.

Kevin Elyot (1951–)

Kevin Elyot is a gay dramatist whose award–wining plays have moved into the mainstream of contemporary British drama. Elyot has made an important, innovative contribution to gay drama in that his characters do not hate being gay. They suffer as other lovers do, they are buffeted by the ignorant, and they endure the wasting and the deaths of lovers and friends, but they do not hate themselves.

Elyot was born in Birmingham. He attended the King Edward's School in that city and then Bristol University. His first produced stage play was *Coming Clean* (1982), which at that relatively early date shocked audiences and reviewers with its male nudity. *The Day I Stood Still* (1998) is set in three scenes spanning the 1960s to the 1990s. It reveals the price of the unrequited love of a gay man for his male friend as time passes. Elyot's best-known drama is *My Night with Reg* (1994). In *Mouth to Mouth* (2001), Frank, a fortyish dramatist suffering from AIDS, reminisces in Proustian fashion about his youth, his relationship with his mother, and the bourgeois world of his childhood.

Elyot has also written successful television plays and a film version of *My Night with Reg*.

M A J O R   P L A Y

My Night with Reg (1994)

My Night with Reg is a tragicomedy informed by AIDS. Three parties take place in Guy's London flat with a few years between each one. The same characters appear in each scene. In the first scene, Guy is preparing a housewarming dinner. The group will be small: Daniel, a friend from Cambridge days, Daniel's partner Reg, and assorted others. The play begins like a typical West End farce, except that the fear of AIDS hangs in the air. There is flirtation and revelations of affairs. John, a young decorator, is having an affair with Reg. In the course of the play it is revealed that everyone in sight has had a one-night stand with Reg except Guy, who has had a very limited sex life.

Reg dies of AIDS, and the question arises: Has Reg infected all his friends and partners? Still, after Reg's funeral there is sexual betrayal by lovers, and despite the gallows humor in the play, all the characters are sadly possessed by their memories of Reg. *My Night with Reg* moves from campy fun and joy in life to deep sorrow.

Additional Reading
Elyot, Kevin. *My Life with Reg*. London: Nick Hern, 2001.

Stephen Poliakoff (1952–)

Stephen Poliakoff is a prophetic playwright who sees little hope for the future of Britain because society is breaking down. Poliakoff's characters are debilitated, dispossessed, and self-destructive people. They are often full of self-contempt, and anxiety is their chief emotion. Off-stage mobs are always waiting to rampage and shed blood. The modern world is concrete-bleak, trash-plastic, unfeeling, and full of terror. For Poliakoff, drama must have social significance or it is worthless. His theater dresses thought.

Poliakoff was born in London. His father, a physicist turned businessman, emigrated to Britain from Russia in 1924. Poliakoff was educated at Westminster School in London. He studied at Kings College, Cambridge, from 1972 to 1973. He was writer-in-residence at the National Theatre from 1976 to 1977. Poliakoff has had an extensive, successful career as a screen and television writer. He married Sandy Welch in 1983. The couple has one child.

Clever Soldiers (1974) is about the privileges that public school graduates had in World War I because of their class. The function of the public school (and the university) was to inculcate a sense of superiority. *Heroes* (1975) shows a government unable to stop armed violence because democracy has eroded away. In *Hitting Town* (1975), an incestuous brother and sister wander through a joyless, sterile, urban wasteland as moral entropy takes its inevitable toll and resistance to decay seems futile. *City Sugar* (1975), a companion play to *Hitting Town*, portrays a radio disk jockey who appears in the prior play disgusted by the sickly, soupy songs he must play to placate and pacify his audience so that they do not think about how awful their lives really are. The disk jockey is an instrument of lowest–common–denominator conformity. *Strawberry Fields* (1977) follows a right-wing extremist group that seems to battle the moral and political breakdown in dried–up ghost towns, but in fact the group is simply a part of the problem, not the solution. Ultimately, young extremists are a danger to themselves.

Favourite Nights (1981) depicts Catherine, a language teacher and an evening escort, struggling to break the bank at a casino so that she does not have to sleep with her German client. The protagonist of *Breaking the Silence* (1984), a wealthy inventor, is named Pesiakoff (close to Poliakoff). Historical events in an unstable Soviet Union just after the 1917 revolution cause him to lose his home and keep moving from place to place, often leaving his family behind, in service to the state. The twentieth century is, after all, the century of the displaced person. *Breaking the Silence* (1984) is Poliakoff's most highly regarded play. It is based on the life of his own grandfather. In it, a wealthy Jewish aristocrat in the Russian revolution plans his escape to England when the state forces him to do meaningless work.

American Days (1997) states that rock music is the message of revolt, while the blues are an attempt to alleviate social pressure for the individual as well as society. *The Summer Party* (1980) uses a rock festival as a metaphor for the controlled violence society permits for the reduction of pressure by angry and dangerous youth. The pampered celebrities and pop-tarts are kept separate, while the audience enjoys thinking they are alive. In *Favorite Nights* (1981), gambling in London casinos helps potentially suicidal people forget that they contribute nothing to society. *Coming to the Land* (1987) is about the trials of a Polish immigrant in Britain, immigration being a subtheme in Poliakoff's work.

Poliakoff deals conceptually with film in *Remember This* (1999). He has become more and more interested in the medium. *Sweet Panic* (2004) shows how a child therapist's world turns to chaos.

Additional Reading
Poliakoff, Stephen. *Plays: One.* London: Methuen Drama, 1989.
——. *Plays: Two.* London: Methuen Drama, 1994.
——. *Plays: Three.* London: Methuen Drama, 1998.

Timberlake Wertenbaker (1955–)

Timberlake Wertenbaker is a leader of the second wave of feminist writers who came after Gems and Churchill. She has written or adapted more than a dozen plays, most of which have been successfully performed. Her playwriting encompasses both the historic and domestic sphere. In both, patriarchy is the source of arbitrary authoritarian control against which her protagonists struggle.

Wertenbaker's dramas reveal two worlds: the public, outdoor world of men that is often violent; and the indoor, private, intimate, and passionate world of women. She indicates that the treatment of women in society is not based on biological attributes, but on male prejudices, which, unfortunately, were and often are endorsed by women. As a result, the contributions that the marginalized could make to society are lost.

Wertenbaker was born in the United States and lived in France, where her early education took place. Later she studied at an American university. She worked as a journalist in London and New York and also taught French in Greece. In 1978 she began her playwriting career with *This Is No Place for Tallulah Bankhead.* Playwriting residencies then followed with the Shared Experience Company in 1984 and the Royal Court Theatre in 1985. Wertenbaker has been working as a playwright, screenwriter, and television writer ever since. She has translated plays by Sophocles, Euripides, Marivaux, and Anouilh.

Case to Answer (1980) and *Abel's Sister* (1984) decry the self-righteousness of people who find convenient ways to avoid translating their idealism into action.

New Anatomies (1981) tells the story of the curious life of Isabelle Eberhardt, a Geneva-born daughter of a Russian anarchist who at the end of the nineteenth century traveled through the deserts of French North Africa and drowned in a flash flood in a remote village. She left behind a journal. The short play is performed by five women, even though there are male characters in it. The twenty-seven-year-old Isabelle—worn out, in ragged Arab male attire (jellaba), nearly toothless, and drunk—narrates the events of her life from childhood on. Wertenbaker is defying the conventions for the portrayal of heroines. Dressed thus, the Arabs accept her; the French do not. Wertenbaker indicates that looking like, and acting like, a man gives women freedom and advantages that dress wearers never have.

In *The Grace of Mary Travers* (1985), a young woman's desire to learn offends her patriarchal father's sense of her social utility and so she rebels. *Our Country's Good* (1988) is based on *The Play-*

maker, a novel by Thomas Keneally about the convict settlement in Australia.

The Love of the Nightingale (1988) is based on the ancient Greek legend of Philomele. Two Athenian sisters, Procne and Philomele, face different futures. The former marries a northern Greek and goes to live in his culture. The latter is content in the safety of the women's world. When Procne has a son, she has her husband, Tereus, travel to Athens to ask her parents to allow Philomele to visit her. Sailing north, Tereus kills the ship's captain, rapes Philomele, and later cuts out her tongue. Procne's son then attacks Philomele too, but is killed by the women of the court. Procne has let violence swirl around her. Individual women are powerless unless they act in consort, and that seldom happens.

Three Birds Alighting on a Field (1991) anatomizes the corrupt world of high-priced art. In *The Break of Day* (1994), based on Chekov's *Three Sisters*, Wertenbaker states that Britain must abandon traditional isolationism and become involved with world problems. *Credible Witness* (2001) is Wertenbaker's latest drama. It is a refugee story in which a Macedonian mother comes to Britain looking for her beloved son whom she is sure the authorities have detained and forgotten about. It is as much about the mythical nature of exile as it is about current treatment of refugees.

M A J O R   P L A Y

Our Country's Good (1988)

Our Country's Good is set in a colony of convicts and guards in Sydney Cove, New South Wales, Australia, in the year 1789. Its subject is the first staging of a European play in Australia. One major theme in the play is the redeeming value of art; another is the liberal belief that human beings treated well will do well. *Our*

Country's Good is a clever, delightful, and charming piece of theater that leaves an audience believing there is good in almost every person, even those who have committed grievous crimes.

Army Lieutenant Ralph Clark wants to be a theater director, and so he valiantly tries to produce a play for the edification and enjoyment of prisoners and guards. His actors will be convicts. The idea is attacked by the officers of the garrison, especially the commanding officer of the marines, Major Ross. Clark is English, so naturally he selects a comedy by the Restoration Irish playwright George Farquhar, *The Recruiting Officer*. As rehearsals progress Clark falls in love with his leading lady, the convict Mary Brenham, and their romance is touching.

The problems of producing a sophisticated piece of London comedy in an eighteenth–century prison colony with convicts as performers are formidable indeed. But with the support of the forward–looking governor of the colony, and despite a raid on the settlement, Clark brings it off. The last words of Wertenbaker's play are the opening lines of Farquhar's.

Wertenbaker's use of language in *Our Country's Good* is particularly effective. She contrasts the honed and balanced lines of Farquhar, a master dramatist, with the slang of the convicts, the dry diction of English gentlemen officers, and the poignant words of the aboriginal observer who is witnessing the beginning of the end of his culture.

Additional Reading
Wertenbaker, Timberlake. *Plays: One.* London: Faber and Faber, 1996.
——. *Plays: Two.* London: Faber and Faber, 2002.

Sarah Daniels (1957–)

Sarah Daniels is primarily concerned with women's issues, and women are always the protagonists in her dramas. Her agit-prop plays are exciting and controversial. Her main subject is the oppression and exploitation of women by men, and in her plays women come to realize how the patriarchal system dominates them. Then they rebel. When they sometimes succeed in their struggles it is because other women–bonding in sisterhood come to their aid.

Daniels was born in London and educated there. Bored with a job after schooling, in 1980, having written a play or two, she answered an ad in *Time Out*, the magazine of the Royal Court Theatre, for submissions of plays by new playwrights. A favorable response by the literary manager launched her playwriting career. Daniels's plays have also been performed in Australia, Asia, North America, and several continental European countries.

In *Ripen our Darkness* (1981), a middle-aged wife of a church warden and mother of three sons, and her lesbian daughter with a lover come to find it impossible to live within the narrow confines of the patriarchal church.

Masterpieces (1985), a powerful drama, is ironically titled because it deals with the social consequences of pornography. A middle-aged couple, Jennifer and Clive, have a married daughter, Rowena, who is a social worker. Her friend Yvonne is a teacher who is disturbed because boys bring pornography to school. Rowena is curious and she asks her husband, Trevor, to bring home some pornography. Then Yvonne and Rowena look at the material and are shocked at the way women are treated in it. It is a crime against women. Rowena takes out her anger first on Trevor, who makes light of women selling their bodies. Then she learns that her father has had a mistress for years even though her mother has played sexual games to get her husband to give up the affair. In a fury, Rowena pushes an unknown man under a train and is tried for murder. For Daniels, society's unwillingness to curb pornography is a crime against all women, and a violent reaction may be irrational but understandable, if not justifiable.

The title of *Neaptide* (1986) refers to the lowest tide in the monthly cycle of the tides. It occurs twice a month when the moon and the sun are in opposition. The play is about the ever-recurring conflict between women and men. *Byrthrite* (1986) discusses how society allows male appropriation of women's bodies in birthing. *Head-Rot Holiday* (1982) concerns women condemned to mental institutions. *Blow Your House Down* (1995) treats the case of the Yorkshire Ripper who terrorized women in northern Britain in the late 1970s. *Best Mates* (2000) was written to be performed alongside canals. In it a young student on a waterways field trip meets a girl who works on a canal boat. He hitches a lift and finds a very a harsh reality and different life without the modern conveniences he is used to.

M A J O R   P L A Y

Neaptide (1986)

Neaptide takes place in London in 1983. Its subject, of vital importance to women, is the way that women are mistreated by the legal system. The play employs–as a bedtime story told to a little girl–the Greek myth about Persephone's abduction and forced marriage. Claire is a lesbian mother and teacher who does not know whether or not she should come out and be a role model because she does not want to risk her position. Also, she is involved in a custody battle with her ex-husband over their daughter, Poppy, who lives with Claire.

In the end Claire loses the custody battle. The father is awarded care and control of Poppy. Desperately, Claire abducts Poppy, and they join Claire's sister in America. But in Britain, and presumably elsewhere, state discrimination against women in court continues.

Additional Reading

Daniels, Sarah. *Plays: One.* London: Methuen Drama, 1991.

———. *Plays: Two.* London: Methuen Drama, 1994.

Sarah Kane (1971–1999)

Sarah Kane was a moralist whose technique was to shock her audience into seeing the starkest realities of life. She passionately believed that political and personal life are inseparable. For her the theater was a part of society, not some external force nudging it. The theater's job is to show the world how it really is. Kane did not make statements. Instead, she lit up points of view.

Sarah Kane had established a reputation as the *enfante terrible* of the British theater before her suicide by hanging at the age of twenty-seven. Kane grew up in Kelvedon Hatch, near Brentwood, Essex. Her mother was a teacher and her father was a journalist for the *Daily Mirror.* Kane embraced her parents' devout Christianity and became evangelical at an early age. She attended Sheffield Comprehensive School, after which she enrolled in Bristol University, receiving a bachelor of arts degree (with honors) in drama in 1992. At Bristol Kane began writing monologues. Her friends at college and later have called her an extremely intense and angry person.

Kane went on to study playwriting for a year with David Edgar at Birmingham University and then moved to London to become a literary associate at the Bush Theatre, where she was given to lecturing actors and directors on sight.

Kane's first play, *Blasted* (1995), a half-naturalistic, half-symbolic work, outraged the audience with its sheer violence: scenes of rape, torture, and mutilation. Men are shown as rapists and cannibalistic sadists. But *Blasted* received instant notoriety. The play is set in an expensive hotel room in Leeds where Ian, a criminal type who claims to be an undercover agent, and Cate, a naive girl, have come for sex. During oral sex she bites his penis. A soldier bursts in and Cate runs out as he urinates on the bed. The hotel is bombed, and in the wreckage the soldier rapes Ian, sucks out and eats his eyes, and then shoots himself. Cate returns with a baby. It dies and is buried under floorboards. Cate goes out to find food, and blind Ian gets under the boards to masturbate, defecate, and eat the baby. Then Ian dies as Kate returns with food. Kane was indicating the reality of the Bosnian war through the landscape of sexual imagination.

Roughly based on Euripide's *Hippolytus* and Racine's *Phaèdre*, Kane's *Phaedre's Love* (1996) begins with Hippolytus watching television, masturbating with one sock and blowing his nose with the other. He is depressed. His young stepmother, Phaedre, performs fellatio on him, but it does not help. He cannot feel anything for her. Leaving a note stating that Hippolytus raped her, she kills herself. An angry mob castrates him and grills his genitals on a barbecue. At the end he seems to have enjoyed his fate. *Phaedre's Love* is less successful than *Blasted* because in Kane's contemporary configuration it is hard to take the tragedy seriously.

Cleansed (1998) is about love and madness, as well as addiction, loss, and suffering. Sexual identity is fluid and sometimes in doubt. Grace and Graham were incestuous, identity–sharing twins, but he is dead and she assumes his identity. Other characters are struggling with addiction to drugs. Horrible, sadistic tortures ensue. Finally, the mutilated, rat–bitten, cross–dressed characters conclude that all activity in life is pointless. As all the characters are young, Kane seems to want to prepare youth for futures that are sure to include trauma and horror.

A poetic, enigmatic, experimental play, *Crave* (1998) has four characters, A, B, C, and M. What they crave is what cripples them emotionally: love. An older man craves a young black woman, and an older woman desires sex with a young man who could father her child. *Crave* is an ambitious attempt to create a new theatrical form with the cascading of poetic images, but the experiment is not successful. Although the play suggests that there is hope for humanity, the plot ends in despair and suicide.

Additional Reading

Kane, Sarah. *Complete Plays*. London: Methuen, 1996.

Saunders, Graham. *Love Me or Kill Me: Sarah Kane and the Theatre of Extremes*. Manchester: Manchester University Press, 2002.

Selected Critical Bibliography

Index

Selected Critical Bibliography

Aston, Elaine, and Janelle Reinelt, eds. *The Cambridge Companion to Modern British Women Playwrights*. Cambridge: Cambridge University Press, 2000.

Bock, Hedwick, and Albert Wertheim. *Essays on Modern British Drama*. Munich: Hueber, 1981.

Bogard, Travis, and William I. Oliver, eds. *Modern Drama: Essays in Criticism*. Oxford: Oxford University Press, 1965.

Bull, John. *New British Political Dramatists*. New York: Grove, 1983.

Clum, John M. *Still Acting Gay: Male Homosexuality in Modern Drama*. New York: St. Martin's, 2000.

Corrigan, Robert W. *The Theatre in Search of a Fix*. New York: Dell, 1973.

Dromgoole, Dominic. *The Full Room: An A to Z of Contemporary Playwriting*. London: Methuen, 2002.

Elsom, John. *Postwar British Theatre*. London: Routledge and Kegan Paul, 1976.

Esslin, Martin. *Theatre of the Absurd*. Garden City, N.Y.: Doubleday, 1961.

Eyre, Richard, and Nicholas Wright. *Changing Stages: A View of British and American Theatre in the Twentieth Century*. New York: Knopf, 2001.

Griffin, Penny. *Arthur Wing Pinero and Henry Jones*. New York: St. Martin's, 1991.

Hayman, Ronald. *British Theatre since 1955*. Oxford: Oxford University Press, 1979.

Houghton, Norris. *The Exploding Stage: An Introduction to Twentieth-Century Drama*. New York: Dell, 1971.

Innes, Christopher. *Modern British Drama, 1890–1990*. Cambridge: Cambridge University Press, 1992.

——. *Modern British Drama: The Twentieth Century.* Cambridge: Cambridge University Press, 2002.

Itzin, Catherine. *Stages in the Revolution: Political Theatre in Britain since 1968.* London: Methuen, 1980.

Kaufmann, R. J., ed. *G. B. Shaw: A Collection of Critical Essays.* Englewood Cliffs, N.J.: Prentice-Hall, 1965.

O'Connor, Sean. *Straight Acting: Popular Gay Drama from Wilde to Rattigan.* London: Cassell, 1998.

Peacock, D. Keith. *Radical Stages: Alternate History in Modern British Drama.* New York: Greenwood, 1991.

Raby, David Ian. *British and Irish Political Drama in the Twentieth Century: Implicating the Audience.* New York: St. Martin's, 1986.

Rebellato, Dan. *1956 and All That: The Making of Modern British Drama.* London: Routledge, 1999.

Reinelt, Janelle. *After Brecht: British Epic Theater.* Ann Arbor: University of Michigan Press, 1994.

Rusinko, Susan. *British Drama 1950 to the Present: A Critical History.* Boston: Twayne, 1989.

Shellard, Dominic. *British Theatre since the War.* New Haven: Yale University Press, 1999.

Sierz, Aleks. *In-Your-Face Theatre: British Drama Today.* London: Faber and Faber, 2001.

Sinfield, Alan. *Out on Stage: Lesbian and Gay Theatre in the Twentieth Century.* New Haven: Yale University Press, 1999.

Taylor, John Russell. *Anger and After.* Rev. ed. Harmondsworth, U.K.: Penguin, 1963.

——. *The Rise and Fall of the Well-Made Play.* New York: Hill and Wang, 1967.

——. *The Second Wave: British Drama of the Sixties.* London: Eyre Methuen, 1971.

Tynan, Kenneth. *Right and Left.* London: Longmans, Green, 1967.

Wandor, Michelene. *Postwar British Drama: Looking Back in Gender.* London: Routledge, 2001.

——. *Understudies: Theatre and Sexual Politics.* London: Eyre Methuen, 1981.

Worth, Katharine J. *Revolutions in Modern English Drama.* London: G. Bell, 1973.

Zeifman, Hersh, and Cynthia Zimmerman, eds. *Contemporary British Drama: Essays from Modern Drama.* Toronto: University of Toronto Press, 1993.

Index